The California Garden

Jere Stuart French

The California Garden

and the Landscape Architects who Shaped it

by

Jere Stuart French

"The garden is the outdoor continuation of the house."
(Inscription at the entry to the Rose Garden, Exposition Park Los Angeles)

Printed in Hong Kong

ISBN 0-941236-19-6

Book Design and Typesetting by Lisa Burkhart

Printed and bound by Dai Nippon Printing Co., Ltd. in Hong Kong

Contents

Acknowledgements

Author's Acknowledgments

The author is indebted to the following people who gave their time, made introductions, offered advise, sent photographs from family collections, and in general provided the support and encouragement to complete this project.

Philip Adams, Sydney Baumgartner, Lisa Burkhart, Ozzie Da Ros,
Kellam de Forest, Bob Fletcher, David Gebhard, Dan Gregory,
Susan Gross Pierson, Grace Hall, Peter Huntsman-Trout, Shirley Kerins,
Jack Moore, Margaret Mori, Joe Rodriguez, Anita Rubalcava, Bob Smaus,
David Streatfield, Paul G. Thiene, James Yoch

The author and the Landscape Architecture Foundation also wish to give special thanks to Julius Schulman for opening his photo library to the book, and for his patience, enthusiasm, and wonderful lunches in his garden with his wife, Olga.

The author gives a very special thanks, as well, to Maggie Baylis for her time, her encouragement, and her financial support for this project.

Thanks are also extended to the California Garden Clubs, Inc., and to individual members who gave assistance and encouragement to the author.

Finally, the author is indebted to Courtland Paul and Peridian for their continuing support and direction. Without their efforts, this book would never have been produced.

Picture Acknowledgments

Julius Schulman, Richard Fish, Charles Ralph, Jere French, Crandall & Crandall, Dana Levy, Dariouche Showghi, Shirley Kerins, Susan Pierson, Dane Williams, Richard Wilson, John Duus, Garrett Eckbo, Robert Royston, Douglas Baylis, Lawrence Halprin, Tom Brown, Theodore Osmundson, Emmet Wemple, Owen Peters, Martin Brinkerhoff, Joseph Yamada, David Walker, Jay Venezi., Sunset Magazine (Darrow M. Watt), Curtice Taylor

Illustration Acknowledgments

Zeki Abed, Maggie Baylis, Mary Carden, Anthony Van Strauhal

Publisher's Acknowledgments

The Landscape Architecture Foundation and the Author are extremely grateful to the following individuals and firms whose financial contributions have enabled the publishing of this book. The funds received were used to pay for the cost of publishing so that all proceeds from the sale of this book will accrue directly to the Foundation so that it may continue its efforts on behalf of the Landscape Architecture profession.

Benefactor
($10,000 or more)
Environmental Industries, Inc.
Peridian

Patron
($5,000—$9,999)
Maggie Baylis
EDAW
Gillespie/DeLorenzo
Anthony M. Guzzardo and Associates, Inc.
Land Concern, Ltd.
Lifescapes
Wimmer/Yamada

Sponsor
($1-$999)
KTU&A
Royston, Hanamoto, Alley and Abbey

The Landscape Architecture Foundation wishes to express its appreciation to the Rainbird and Toro Endowements for their financial assistance. In addition, the Foundation is deeply indebted to Burton Sperber and Environmental Industries for their financial assistance which was given at the book's inception.

To my Wife

Joan

Preface

The California garden is an enclosed space, an outdoor room, attached to the house, to its functions and activities, but separate just the same. The walls may be stone, or any other structural material. They may also be shrubs, potted plants and planters, or neatly trimmed hedges. Trees, awnings, arbors, along with the everchanging cloud patterns above us, are the ceiling, and the floor can be anything suitable for walking or sitting—tile, brick, aggregate, gravel, grass.

We use our California garden as we would any room. It is private, useful and, we trust, attractive. It serves our many needs, and in times of growing costs and shrinking lot sizes, it is a means of making our lives more peaceful, more balanced.

Introduction

By Julius Schulman

Here in my garden in West Los Angeles, I grow a myriad of succulents and aloes. For an article I wrote and illustrated many years ago for *Woman's Day* magazine, I demonstrated that succulents are so abundant in their blossoming that in my garden I have plants which can flower in every month in their characteristic nature. From the onset of my garden program, 1950, and continuously ever since, I have recreated the qualities which were so indelibly imprinted on my childhood. My continuous planting of numerous trees, mostly conifers, has resulted in a forest-like view wherever my paths traverse. In a quiet mini-canyon at the edge of my land, I planted seedling redwoods in 1959, which are now seventy-five feet tall!

I have experienced in my garden, without consideration of the many rules and instructions thrown at the amateur gardener, azaleas blossoming for months on end. We do not feed them nor measure the chemical nature of the soil. Perhaps those attempting to create a garden would do well to meet with a landscape architect and together explore the infinite variety of magical plant materials available. As in my garden of redwoods, I can walk down a path and find myself in an open native plant hillside where the sage, buckwheat, wintergreen, scrub oak, and yucca live side by side in a profusion of jade, which I have combined with agaves and aloes to create a fire resistant mass of fresh green. Plants are sociable and do well with an assortment of what are too frequently considered to be competitors. In December, the jade is a mass of blossoms while the sage, often inhabiting the same area, is just beginning to thrust up new, scented leaves!

Can this book be construed as a catalyst, verily as a time machine to function as a directive instrument? A rose garden can be more than a delight, but there are infinite other considerations in the wings. And the wings of birds are to be considered too. I have counted more than eighty species of birds, which have found their way to the richness of food and shelter abundant in my paradise.

A careful reading of Jere French's thorough and colorful research of California's garden history will lead to a feeling of respect for the early explorers who first identified with the wonders of our climate so many years ago, who learned from the Indians the wonders of the native plants. What a remarkable foundation for elevating one's taste in the creation of a genuine California garden.

When I roam along my pine needle strewn paths, my feelings of respect soar in appreciation of the infinite potential which can be achieved by thoughtful design and the selection of plant material. At early hours of dawn, or at dusk, I encounter deer drinking from the pools among the redwoods, and at night the howling of coyotes breaks the silence. In the evening, racoons peer at us through glass walls. What happy moments these are—a full existence created by man and nature.

Los Angeles, 1992

Opposite: Julius Schulman garden.

I.

Shadows and Reflections

'Where bowers of flowers bloom in the sun,
Each morning, at dawning,
Birdies sing and everything

California Here I Come'

Al Jolson and Bud deSilva, 1924

California's yellow iris.

Opposite: Gateway to a Pasadena patio.

garden is a wondrous place, wreathed in the colors of sunlight, the sounds and movements of nature, surrounded always by a veil of our imagination's making, an ever-changing, enchanting place.

Childhood is nourished by a garden where trolls, elves, and fairies dwell. Real frogs watch benignly from mossy banks as spellbound young listeners hear tales of frog princes in the cool of a summer afternoon. A first kiss is stolen in a garden, and under the spell of night-blooming jasmine, promises are whispered with a fingernail moon as witness. Under a bower of climbing yellow roses, the promises are kept.

We eat breakfast in the garden on a Saturday morning in June, wearing an old terrycloth bathrobe over pajamas. On a red-tiled patio surrounded by clay pots of pink and lavender petunias, we attend a garden reception. Balancing plates of canapes and goblets of California zinfandel, we congratulate a young couple or reminisce with old friends. On a Sunday in August, we grill hamburgers and drink cold Mexican beer. Gloves and a baseball appear or a lively discussion commences involving the merits of the Dodgers and the Giants.

In cooler weather, we take our coffee or tea into the garden wrapped in the warmth of a low-lying southern sun that filters through the branches of an old California live oak. A soft western breeze brings a hint of California Bay leaves, sage, or lemon verbena.

This Pasadena home all but disappears within the enclosure of its garden, providing privacy, shade, and seclusion while at the same time welcoming visitors. This landscape has been designed over the years by its owner, Mary Alice Frank.

With the return of the rainy season, we notice the first hyacinth pushing through the moist soil, the newly metamorphosed monarch butterfly pausing to pump its wings atop the curled calla lily, the heavy aroma of orange blossoms, the ripening loquats, and the chirp of the house finch searching the twigs of the elm for the plumpest seeds. Rain washes the dust from the toyon leaves and the fresh scent in the garden spurs us to activity.

We Californians rank high as garden lovers. We know that a long growing season and our moderate Mediterranean climate affords us an extraordinary variety of available plants and an abundance of flowers. And we have become accustomed to outdoor living and to gardens that can accommodate our interests all year long. Our garden is our living room when friends come to call. We read, write letters to less fortunate eastern relations, compose sonnets, and try to organize the week ahead. We play croquet and badminton with our kids on an overworked patch of Bermuda grass, and, when they become teen-agers, we escape from them...into the garden.

We maintain our privacy here, with considered care. A hedge, a decorative fence, a tall shrub border, and a vine-covered wall all serve to increase our garden's capacity for sun bathing, hot tubbing, swimming, or simple solitude. Under a California pepper tree's enclosing branches, we sling a hammock pro-

Above and Opposite: Laguna Beach residence, Greg Grisamore, landscape architect.

dens on our living room walls. We read poems about gardens and listen to romantic songs that recall images: "When the deep purple falls over sleepy garden walls." [1]

Islamic belief envisions paradise—the final resting place—as a garden, not a cemetery, but heaven itself. Placing the beginning of human life in a garden—Eden—is a felicitous and lovely idea. The Hanging Gardens of Babylon and other real or mythical gardens of the past remain a refuge for human imagination. Our own garden, despite the realities of weeds and insects, surely possesses a measure of that selfsame enchantment only time and dedication can produce.

Paintings of gardens and romantic landscapes have, in turn, guided the hands of garden designers. The watercolorist depicts a pair of lovers gliding along a stream in a shallow boat, enjoying a picnic lunch under a tree, or we see an old wooden hay cart rounding the bend of a rocky path. We wonder what lies downstream from the lovers or beyond the bend in the path.

In the same way, we design our gardens to give them mystery, to inspire wonder about what might lie beyond the hedgerow or the screen of papyrus plants. The garden is thus defined by its enclosing agents which give it both form and purpose. But these outdoor rooms are not plastered or painted cubicles. Instead, they are spaces enlivened by the ingenuity of design, as well as the passing of time with infinitely more varied and textured surfaces than paint or wallpaper could ever achieve. It is in this respect, the creating of private and functional outdoor rooms by use of shrubs, fences, retaining walls, decks, and trees, that the California garden achieves a special place in the history of the American garden.

tected from the leaf drop by a bit of awning and sleep in our garden. Dining room, den, study, and family room, the garden is reserved especially for life's pleasant and even passionate pastimes. Here in our garden, we do everything that's fun. And yes, we even garden.

Our California garden draws from a rich heritage of myth and religion, as well as from a history of gardening practices throughout the moderate climes of the world. Historians as early as Pliny and Vitruvius, as well as painters, poets, and philosophers have long described the ameliorative effects of the garden on the human spirit. We find garden themes depicted on rugs, wallpaper, vases, and stained glass; we hang pictures of gar-

Spanish Roots

Just as California's colonial history differs from that of most of eastern United States, so does its garden history. From Massachusetts to Georgia on west to the Mississippi River, the influences of English, Dutch, and French garden styles prevailed throughout much of our early history. Four distinct seasons and temperate climate provided the basis for continuing the established design themes of conquering European powers.

California's history is, of course, quite different. The Spanish adventurers who arrived in the late eighteenth century came to California by way of Mexico, where they had been experiencing cultural blending for nearly three hundred years. To understand how California differed in colonial times from eastern United States, we must first understand the role of the Spanish and their missionary system, a system which led to the founding of mission gardens, adobe ranchos, and the life-style of the old *Californio* communities of the pastoral era. It was in Old California that the concept of the garden as an outdoor room came into being.

From the earliest times, the California garden was a patio, an enclosed space essential to the mission complex, as well as to the adobe ranch house. In the mild climate of southern California, living and working out of doors for much of the year is possible and even preferable. It is also a tradition derived from Spain and Persia, reinforced through Mexican experience. It is a garden history based on the concept of garden as space—a functioning room—instead of an abstract luxury.

California's garden history is also affected by the subsequent arrival of American immigrants. Initially they came in search of adventure and gold, but stayed on to become farmers and citizens of the new land. Their plowed fields, wooden houses, and bedding gardens quickly replaced much of the old Spanish and Mexican architecture and style of the garden. Early in the present century, however, Californians looked again to their Mediterranean roots, to Spain, Persia, and Italy in search of gardens they deemed more appropriate to California living.

Climate
and
Topography

The California garden is shaped by an even stronger factor: climate. We have learned a great deal from people who have developed their societies in the warm, arid places of the world, and we have also managed to ignore many local peculiarities of our natural environment— to our considerable regret. Understanding the climate of California, both north and south, first requires setting aside notions of traditional weather patterns, including such things as summer rainstorms, icy winter winds, and four distinct seasons.

California's climate is not unchanging and monotonous, as visitors from Boston like to report. It is greatly varied by a number of factors: the Japanese current, which warms the Pacific Ocean as it reaches our coastline; the presence of moisture-laden air and its generally moderating effects; the greater temperature ranges and lack of humidity in the inland valleys behind the coastal ranges; and the extremes of temperature variation recorded in the dry, desert climate to the east of the principal north-south mountain chain.

Southern California is defined topographically by three principal transverse mountain ranges, the Santa Ynez, San Gabriel, and San Bernardino Mountains, extending from Point Conception eastward into the deserts.

A coastal landscape near San Luis Obispo.

Elevations in the state vary from 14,000 feet at Mt. Whitney down to more than 100 feet below sea level in Death Valley and the Salton Sea, giving California the highest and lowest elevations in the continental United States. California has five distinct life zones:

Coastal region is marked by cool summers, mild winters, moist air, and normally little rainfall.

Coastal valleys have warmer summers, cooler winters than the coastal zone and more rainfall, averaging eleven to fifteen inches annually. Coastal valleys are drained westerly to the Pacific Ocean by three principal rivers: the Los Angeles, Santa Ana, and San Diego.

Inland valleys are semiarid and separated topographically from the coast by scattered, low-lying north-south ranges. Rainfall here is ten inches or less. Summers are hot and dry, winters cool to chilly.

Deserts, divided by the transverse ranges into the Mojave (high desert) and Colorado (low desert), experience no more than five to ten inches of rain each year. These desert regions are climatically distinct; the Mojave is colder in the winter, with the Joshua tree as its principal plant species, while the Colorado conforms more to the stereotype of a desert, with long, desolate vistas and seemingly endless stands of saguaro cactus.

Mountains, with peaks of more than 10,000 feet, have mild, pleasant summers and cold winters. Precipitation includes snow during winter and spring, a major source of our state's water supply. Thundershowers throughout the summer months are common. Mountain elevations control and determine the extent of the life zones and their climates. The Peninsular Range (the north-south mountains that extend from the Baja Peninsula into San Diego County) separate the Colorado Desert from the southern coastal plain. Except for the deserts and mountains, southern California enjoys a Mediterranean climate of warm, dry summers and mild, moist winters.

California

Physiographic Regions

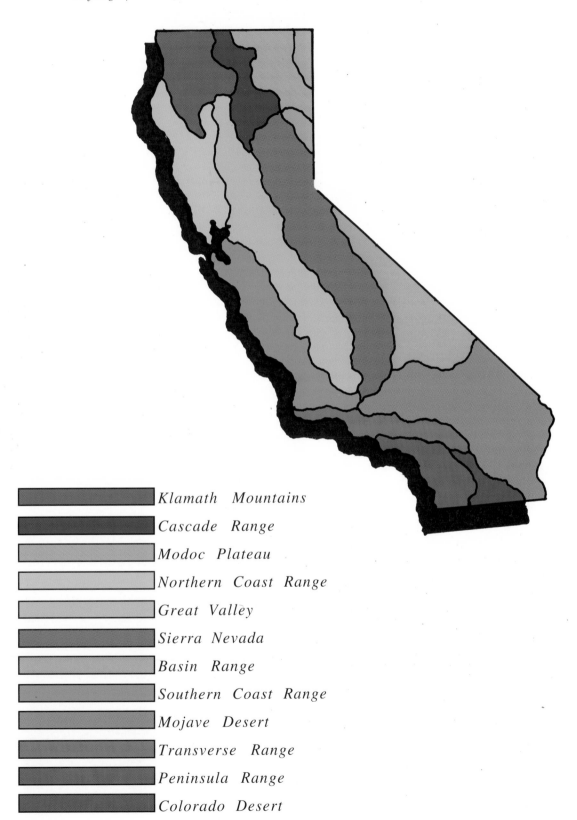

Klamath Mountains
Cascade Range
Modoc Plateau
Northern Coast Range
Great Valley
Sierra Nevada
Basin Range
Southern Coast Range
Mojave Desert
Transverse Range
Peninsula Range
Colorado Desert

North of the transverse ranges, the state is divided topographically into four distinct zones running from west to east: the coastal ranges; the San Joaquin Valley, which extends from Bakersfield northward beyond Redding; the Sierra Nevada Mountains; and below their eastern slope, the Basin Ranges, which represent the westernmost extension of the Great Basin into California.

The coastal zone, north of Point Conception, is cool and moist through most of the summer. Above San Francisco in the Klamath Range, it becomes much cooler year round and is very humid. The north coast is marked by heavy mists and fog throughout much of the year, but about ten miles inland from the sea, a sudden, almost dramatic climatic change occurs. The warmer and drier continental air mass collides with the cool marine air, sending it upward and back out to sea in a continuing revolving pattern. To the east beyond the coastal ranges, the San Joaquin Valley is uniformly hot and dry in summer, cool in winter. The Sierra Nevada Range is cool and pleasant in summer, cold to very cold in winter. Northward, it gradually diminishes into a series of broad, low north-south ranges to the Oregon border.

Most of the northern coast and the San Joaquin Valley are also characterized by a Mediterranean climate defined by two seasons, wet and dry. In the north, particularly along the coast above San Francisco, the amount of rainfall can be more than double that of the southern coastal zone, but the rainy season has approximately the same duration throughout the state—from November to May. In some years, the advent of the rainy season is delayed by local weather conditions until after the first of the year. The amount of rainfall can vary greatly from year to year, as we experienced in the long drought cycle from

1986 to 1992. Generally though, Los Angeles receives ten to fifteen inches of rain, San Francisco gets about double that. When precipitation falls below these norms for several succeeding years, serious drought conditions result and water conservation programs may be mandated throughout the state, as we experienced in the late 1980s. The opposite may occur during seasons of El Niño, when wind reversals across the breadth of the Pacific Ocean can drop torrential storms over much of the Pacific coast during the winter.

Unlike the climatic zones of the midwest and eastern seaboard, the growing season for native plant life occurs in late winter and spring in California. Once the rains begin, the yellow-brown hills rapidly change to emerald green, and soon thereafter, golden poppies, purplish-blue to pale white lupine, and tall yellow mustard begin to clothe the coastal valleys in long veils of color. Soon the dormant shrubbery comes to life and the foothills are instantly aglow in a bluish haze of ceanothus and other colorful chaparral plants that wait only for the arrival of the rain to begin life anew.

A California spring, with flowering barberry, ceanothus and wild current (opposite left). Pampas grass (opposite right), Baby blue eyes and blue-eyed grass (above).

By May, when the rains disappear and the dry season commences, the hillsides once again revert to a bronzy gold. The flower heads of the perennials have become stiff and brittle and are prone to brush fire, as are the yellow grasses on the lower slopes. The most common of the chaparral plants—ceanothus, buckwheat, bladderpod, and chamise—go dormant for the six months of drought that lie ahead, whereas in the foothills and inland valleys a few shrubby trees—toyon, scrub oak, lemonade berry—manage to provide the chaparral zone with some greenery. Named for the chaparro, a scrub oak that grows throughout the dry hillsides of Mexico and a generic term for plants that tolerate drought conditions, our chaparral puzzles new arrivals to California, who are confounded by this reversal of growing seasons. The chaparro also lends its name to the leather pants (chaps) worn by early California vaqueros to protect their legs against its tough, thorny branches. A number of Old California Spanish words found their way, in corrupted form, into the English of arriving Yankees, for example, "Hoosegow" from *juzgado* (judged), and "lariat" from *la riata* (the rope).

Higher up the hillsides into protected valleys and north-facing ravines where the summer sun is less intense and groundwater more abundant, we will begin to find live oaks, a few low-altitude conifers, and in the stream-fed valleys where water may run throughout the dry season, we find sycamore, California bay, alder, and maple.

The overland settlers who came to California in the 1840s from St. Louis and other eastern embarkation points showed little interest in these native plants of California. Like the mission fathers before them, the new settlers brought their own plants and farming practices, along with their particular aesthetic and cultural values. Unlike the mission fathers, however, they took little notice of native plant material or the indigenous farming practices.

To this day, many Californians remain unfamiliar with most native plants, uncertain of the growing season, unprepared for the two-season climate. Despite recent efforts to popularize the use of natives in garden design, nurseries continue to stock predominantly European, Asiatic, and traditional eastern American plants; plants that are better suited to the temperate zones of the world, where winters are bitter cold and summers wet. Not only do these *exotics* require constant nurturing—water, fertilizing, and acid soil treatments—but some of them have been shown to add

measurably to atmospheric carbon dioxide levels. Studies at the University of California, Riverside, in 1992 demonstrated exceedingly high emission levels of carbon dioxide from carrotwood *(Cupaniopsis anacardioides)* and sweetgum *(Liquidambar styraciflua).*

Some introduced species, especially those from Mediterranean climates like our own, acclimate to local conditions and many readily naturalize in California. Plants from Australia and New Zealand, for example, have helped to expand the garden designer's palette, and the introduction of certain commercial imports such as citrus fruit, table and wine grapes, olives, almonds, apricots, kiwi fruit, and various nut trees have contributed to the state's economic prosperity. One of the few notable commercial failures is the eucalyptus, which was imported to Cali-

fornia from Australia and planted in large numbers along the coast and in inland valleys during the late nineteenth century. Although it failed to provide the railroad companies with much-needed lumber for ties or the building industry with construction-grade lumber as intended, it has succeeded, in its many and varied species, to provide shade, color, and character to California gardens and open spaces.

Canyon live oak (opposite), California poppies blooming in April (above) .

The Franciscan missionaries brought large numbers of cuttings and seed with them from Mexico. These plants had proven their usefulness and adaptability in the harsh climatic conditions of the Sonoran Desert and the Baja Peninsula. By using plants familiar to them, they were exceedingly successful in coaxing productivity from the California soil. Later settlers were also pleased to discover how well everything grew in the rich earth of California, in spite of the lack of sufficient water. In mission and *rancho* gardens, native plants were commonplace as well, thanks to the knowledge and assistance of the local Indians who explained their varied uses. In this way, toyon, California bay, wild cherry, yucca, agave, and prickly pear cactus all became standard medicinal products of the missions. With Indian help, mainly through Indian labor, complex irrigation systems were constructed to bring water from nearby creeks to the mission gardens.

Life in California in the early nineteenth century was not easy for the Spanish settlers; they came to depend on local knowledge and local plant materials, many of which still retain their Spanish names: *encino* (live oak), *aliso* (California sycamore), *fresno* (evergreen ash), *álamo* (poplar, alder), *nogal* (California walnut), and *sauce* (willow).

Water-delivery systems have certainly changed greatly from the days of the mission gardens, but water availability has become more of a problem for California gardeners with each passing year, each new housing tract. Depending on the plants we select, the design itself, and how much we have

learned from the past, our garden may require less water than our neighbor's. Technology has vastly changed the way we do things, but we can still learn from the practices of these early settlers who managed to survive and even thrive in those simpler times.

This is the story of our garden heritage from mission gardens and the enclosed rancho patios of early California, through the era of the great estates and Mediterranean revival, beyond the space-conscious modern garden that developed during and after World War II, to the present status of the California garden and its future, as well as its effect on public and commercial institutions in the state.

It is also the story of the men and women who have helped to make the California garden the romantic, unique, enduring, and useful place that it is.

Opposite: Corredor at the Pala Asistencia

II.

Gardens of Old California

Pudimos penetrar en el patio cuadrado, rodeado de arquería en cuyo centro se desgranaba una fuente (Through the door we entered a square patio, enclosed by an arcade, in whose center a fountain bubbled.)

Pensativa, Jesus Goytortúa, 1947

Fountain at San Diego Mission

Opposite: California Historical Society, Santa Barbara.

Driving California One today, north from Santa Barbara between Morro Bay and Monterey, we experience few of the hardships of the first Spanish adventurers. But in passing through that magnificent coastal landscape of high ridges, steep cliffs, rushing streams that crash down in occasional waterfalls from the rugged seaside slopes, and deep-forested glens of Monterey pine and cypress, we can try to imagine their awe, their bewilderment. Unlike the pallid, arid coast of Mexico, this was truly a new land.

The Spanish settlement of California had, however, an inauspicious beginning. On April 11, 1769, a battered wooden ship limped into what is now San Diego harbor, and the sick and starving crew disembarked onto sandy flats near the present location of the city's airport. They had spent fifty-one frightening and miserable days sailing from San Lucas, near the tip of the Baja California peninsula. The tiny, ill-provisioned vessel continually fought head winds that had driven them off course and out into the open sea. Built by unskilled Indian labor out of scavenged lumber, its hardware and anchor having been carried over the mountains from Mexico City to the coast, this rough craft was the anointed vehicle for Spain's final adventure in the new world...the conquest of California.

No one came to the shore to greet the little band of survivors. No indigenous people watched curiously from the surrounding bluffs as the exhausted crew pulled themselves onto the barren strand of beach, to regain strength and to wait.

The rugged coastline of San Luis Obispo County.

Food and water, not Indian attack, would be their immediate problem as they waited for the arrival of another small boat and two land parties, including the expedition's leaders, Gaspar de Portolá and Father Junípero Serra. Both had elected to walk to California, having observed the construction of the sea vessels and their preparations.

The expedition's principal goal, however, was not the harbor at San Diego, but a place further north, which had been described in detail by Sebastiano Vizcaino in 1602 and named in honor of Mexico's viceroy at the time, the Count of Monterey. Here, according to that intrepid explorer's account, was not only a marvelous harbor, but also a land rich in resources with great stands of trees for lumber, abundant wild game, and ample fresh water running from countless streams. It should prove an easy matter to discover this harbor, the report concluded, as there was a magnificent oak tree spreading its huge branches over the precise spot where a port could be built.

History has recorded that Portolá was a stern, enduring soldier, stubborn, narrow of mind but obedient to orders, as his statue in modern Monterey's touristed harbor suggests. Having reached the lower arm of San Francisco Bay, which he rejected for lack of an oak, Portolá eventually located Monterey Bay. On June 3, 1770, Father Serra stood under the branches of the old oak and commenced the establishment of the California mission system. Eventually twenty-one missions would be founded, each about a day's journey apart, stretching from the original landfall in San Diego to Sonoma.

Right: Statue of Gaspar de Portolá Monterey.

Above: Mission San Fernando Rey de España as it looked in 1875. Restoration efforts, begun by Charles Lummis in 1916, were eventually completed during the 1950s.

Opposite: Ruins of Mission San Luis Rey de Francia, near Oceanside, as it appeared about 1880. Roofing joists and other wood members were stripped from the mission after secularization for use in building the adobe ranchos of newly arriving Mexican settlers, after 1834. Nearby Guajome Adobe is an example.

The primary task of the Franciscan fathers was to christianize the various indigenous people who were living at the time within the established mission territories, changing, irrevocably, the lives of these California Indian tribes. By the end of the first decade of colonization, eight missions had been founded, with forty Spanish padres directing the lives of over 40,000 Indian converts.

The second obligation of the mission program was to grow food for the mission populations, in addition to the military garrisons planned for Monterey and elsewhere. From the missions in Baja California, the padres were supplied with cuttings of a variety of fruit trees—pomegranate, citrus, almond, apricot, peach, pear, walnut, cherry, and plum—that had proven resistant to the heat and alkali soils. All of these fruits had come to Mexico over several centuries from Spain, and the Jesuit fathers who pre-

ceded the Franciscans there had learned to graft and to make rooted cuttings to be wrapped in leaves and cotton to keep them moist during the long journey north. In addition, grapes, strawberries, and olive plants were shipped to Monterey and San Diego or carried by foot from the Baja missions. Many ornamentals were also introduced into mission gardens this way, making them

colorful, as well as useful centers for the spread of Spanish authority in the new colony. With the help of the local Indian converts, the padres learned to make use of many native California plants, including sage, chia, pennyroyal, yucca, agave, and native strawberry and grape. The padres also raised acres of useable crops: corn, lentils, garbanzos, wheat, and cotton, for the most part.

All of the missions maintained large tracts of land for grazing, as well as for cultivation. In time, they were able to meet the demands for food in the sparsely settled colony. Supplies that had to be imported from Mexico, such as hardware, clothing, and all manufactured goods, arrived infrequently at Monterey or San Diego. Supplying Alta California's requirements, particularly the need for additional settlers and families to develop the planned towns, continually grew

more difficult as everything had to be transported from Acapulco to La Paz and then, by way of a long and difficult journey, to San Diego and Monterey.

Opposite: Mission San Juan Capistrano. The central courtyard and fountain as it appeared in this 1930 photo.

Below and Opposite Bottom: The entry garden and arcade of Mission San Miguel Arcangel, founded in 1797. Missions were responsible for raising food for the Spanish colony, as well as bringing the indigenous population under Christian protection and control.

Anza's Trail

Several attempts to establish a land route to Alta California failed, mainly because of the impassable wastes and mud flats of the Colorado River delta which lay directly over the pathway from mainland Mexico. With all traffic to Alta California initiated from the southern tip of the Baja peninsula, easterly routes had to be developed to keep supplies and communication moving. Juan Bautista de Anza, a captain in command of the dusty little frontier post of Tubac in the Sonoran Desert of southern Arizona, volunteered to search out such a route. He petitioned the viceroy for permission to attempt the journey from Tubac to Monterey...a distance of more than 900 miles.

When Anza reached the Colorado River on February 7, 1774, he was confronted with a confusing series of meandering streams and broad wetlands which, at that time, formed the upper delta regions of the river's mouth. Attempting to cross this vast *ciénega* (marsh), he became hopelessly lost and was forced to abandon the effort.

Standing at Yuma today where Anza followed the Gila River to its confluence with the Colorado River, a modern traveler would have difficulty in comprehending the problems encountered by those early trail blazers, but journals of nineteenth century travelers describe the Gila as a broad, timber lined river that joined the Colorado in a wide marshy plain filled with willow and cottonwood.

On his second attempt to cross the river into what is now California, Anza was accompanied the following year by a Franciscan friar, Pedro Font, who has left us a wonderfully descriptive account of that journey, particularly in respect to the plant life encountered and its potential use to future settlers. Font had been selected as scribe for the expedition because of his scientific knowledge. According to his accounting of events, it was due to his persistence that they crossed in an upstream direction, rather than allow themselves to be carried south into the delta region, as had happened on Anza's earlier attempt. On entering the Santa Ana River valley on December 31, 1775, Font noted in his journal:

"In the first and second range of hills and their canyons, which are of moist earth, I saw an abundance of rosemary and other fragrant plants, and in the second long canyon many sunflowers in bloom and grape vines and wild grapes of such good stock that it looked like a vineyard; and perhaps with a little cultivation they would yield good grapes. In short, all the country looks good and if the small hills which are in the valleys only had some trees there would be nothing more to desire." [2]

San Juan Bautista Mission garden, euryops blooming.

Father Font's wild grape would probably have been our native grape, *Vitus girdiana*, which was commonly found in the inland valleys of California before cultivation and grazing. He may have mistaken native purple sage for the equally aromatic rosemary. He would also have noticed an abundance of buckwheat, lupine, lemonade berry, and wild rose on the hillsides. Still, this time of year has very little in bloom yet, although sunflowers blooming in December can still surprise visitors to California. His reference to the scarcity of trees is puzzling; the inland valleys of the Santa Ana would certainly have provided willow and in protected areas sycamore and live oak groves. With the cattle that Anza brought on this expedition, the native grasses would disappear in a few decades replaced by invasive grasses that came with the stock animals.

Anza's second expedition, numbering 240 colonial families and soldiers, arrived in San Gabriel on January 5, 1776 and rested there at the recently established mission, where Font made the following entry in his journal:

"The mission has plentiful live oaks and other trees for building timber, and consequently there is abundant firewood...in the creek, celery and other plants that look like lettuce and some roots that look like parsnips grow naturally, and nearby there are turnips, which took possession of the land. And near the site of the old mission, which is distant from the new one about a league (three miles) to the south, there is a country which, as Father Paterno says, looks like the promised land." [3]

Some form of wild parsnip and turnip, of doubtful food value, are known in the western United States, but the lettuce referred to by Font is probably Miner's lettuce (*Montia perfoliata*), relished by Indians and settlers alike. Many such edible native plants still grow in the mountain streams of the Sierra foothills.

Anza's instructions from the viceroy in Mexico City included finding an inland route to Monterey, and from there to San Francisco Bay where a new mission was to be established, together with a garrison for the defense of the newly discovered natural port. The expedition reached the mission in San Luis Obispo in February, and with little more than a pause, it went on to Monterey where they were warmly welcomed. He took his colony—which had grown by two (one death, three births)—the final one hundred miles to the bay, and on March 28, 1776, he stood on the bluff overlooking the Golden Gate, the vast bay, the island, and potential harbors. Standing beside him, Father Font surveyed the scene in awe, later recording:

"The mesa affords a delightful view, for from it one sees a large part of the port...and of the sea all that the eye can take in...indeed, although in my travels I saw very good sites and beautiful country, I saw none that pleased me so much as this...it has the best advantages for founding in it a most beautiful city." [4]

The next day, while scouting the peninsula for mission and garrison sites, Font described the landscape:

San Juan Capistrano Mission

42

"Passing through wooded hills and over flats with good lands, in which we encountered two lagoons and some springs of good water, with plentiful grass, fennel, and other useful herbs, we arrived at a beautiful arroyo which, because it was Friday of Sorrows (Good Friday), we called it the Arroyo de Los Dolores. On its banks we found much and very fragrant manzanita and other plants, and many wild violets." [5]

Anza's choice for a future garrison (*presidio*) on the northernmost tip of the peninsula was strategically correct, if nonetheless, a windy and virtually treeless site. Little was changed in this regard until occupation by the United States after 1846. Later, following his failures during the Civil War, Major General Irvin McDowell became commanding officer at the *presidio* of San Francisco, and redeemed his wartime blunders in part by planting a forest of blue gum eucalyptus, Monterey cypress, and Monterey pine throughout the 1400 acres of the old Spanish garrison. Today these three species continue to dominate the *presidio's* skyline.

In the summer of 1781, after only five years of successful usage, the Anza trail came under heavy attack by Yuma Indians and was closed to further immigration. The flow of settlers north slowed to a trickle, and the sparsely populated enclaves of Alta California grew even more isolated, more independent of the viceroy's rule. A high birthrate amongst the colonists compensated for the loss of immigrants, and by the end of the next decade (1781-90), a new breed of self-reliant, free thinking, individualistic, and democratically spirited folk were beginning to emerge in the new land. They called themselves *Californios*, and they were to prove to be a rather unique society in the Spanish New World.

Rancho Gardens

The homes of the early Spanish settlers in California were simple, rough structures built of sun-dried mud bricks, laced with straw or grass for strength and sized for easy lifting—about a foot by two feet, and six inches or so in thickness. Hand formed and left in the sun to dry, they were later made from wood templates—as they are today in adobe restorations. A coating of wet mud was slathered over both walls inside and out, for insulation and to seal cracks. Windows were small and lacked glass, but were often fitted with wooden grilles and the roofs were flat, the horizontal beams covered with bundled tule rushes, tarred to make them waterproof. During the long hot dry season of southern California, the tar (*brea*) would melt and run down the reed stalks, while during the rainy season, the water would find many opportunities to enter.

Opposite: Rancho La Brea, built in 1828 by Antonio Rocha, was located near Fairfax Avenue in Los Angeles. Before its destruction, it served the early silent movie industry, as in "The Four Horsemen of The Apocalypse." The patio and well (opposite bottom) 1936.

Below: Patio of the Charles Lummis home, Los Angeles, showing a well and California sycamore in this 1930 photo. The garden was restored using water conserving plants favored by Lummis, who for many years was city editor of the **Los Angeles Times.**

These early adobe houses were single story with dirt floors and no fireplaces, or any ventilation beyond the small windows. Usually there were no interior walls, the house being essentially one large room. The door was merely a cowhide flap which one pulled aside to enter. Wood was scarce, especially in the south, and hardware almost nonexistent. Lacking even handmade nails, the roof beams, joists, and tule reeds were lashed together with leather thongs—a commodity becoming more and more commonplace in the rancho economy.

None of these early houses remains standing today, and we must satisfy our curiosity from drawings and a few old photos. By the end of the century, a few improvements had added to their livability: houses were larger, and interior walls were added to create bedrooms and a family living room *(sala)*. In time, a second story was added to houses of the more important *dons*, but, the interior stairways were rather harder to achieve. By far, the most significant addition was the patio. It was here that family gatherings, meals, and all-important occasions would be held. The patio was to become the workplace, the dining room, and the living room for the family, their many guests and visitors. As time went by, the patio grew in size and structure, developing into the center of life for *Californio* society. Designed after antecedents in Andalusia, the California patio was

usually enclosed on at least three sides and might contain a central well or even a fountain, as well as a vine-covered arbor (*ramada*) and plants in clay pots for decoration and household needs. Unless another place was provided for it, all cooking was done here as well—in a beehive-shaped oven. Herb gardens were also cultivated, and chickens usually ranged freely.

Above: Restoration of the Santa Barbara presidio, in process. Volunteers make adobe bricks out of local clay and straw in the courtyard near partially restored quarters and chapel. Completion of the entire presidio will necessitate interruption of two downtown Santa Barbara streets, an unlikely event at present.

Left: Patio of the Santa Barbara Historical Society, a reconstruction of a typical adobe ranch and enclosed patio of tamped earth, well, and fruit trees.

Opposite: The adobe house of Doña Luiz Vigare, located until its destruction on South Ramona Avenue in San Gabriel. A great-granddaughter of a mission soldier, Doña Luiz continued to live here until the late 1930s. Remnants of the original patio, including these drought-tolerant plants, still served the family at the time of this 1936 photo.

There would usually be a veranda (*corredor*) running the length of the walls where doors to the bedrooms and to the sala would be found. The *corredor* was usually a narrow wooden porch that stepped down into the patio. By this time, wood floors had been added to the interiors. A projecting roof gave shade to the *corredor*, where family members could often be found during the heat of the afternoon. The dark, musty interior of the house, with its low ceiling, tiny windows, poor ventilation and light, was good for sleeping, storage—little else. Thus, from the very beginning of what was to become California's pastoral era, the life-style revolved around the patio.

Because most of these households had an abundance of Indian servants, the pleasure-seeking *rancheros* and their families spent most of their time socializing at the frequent fiestas—saints days, weddings and engagements, gatherings of one kind or another—to interrupt the idyllic, if somewhat unchanging daily routine of living. Such occasions were always held in the enclosed patios that afforded a convivial atmosphere for dining, social

interchange, music and dance—the lively and audacious *fandango* for weddings and the like or less boisterous dances for other occasions. Weddings in particular brought out the largest assemblages and the lengthiest programs. Richard Henry Dana described a wedding reception in January, 1836, that lasted for three days in the patio of Juan de la Guerra's Santa Barbara home. Although the *fandango* did not personally please him, Dana notes that it continued well into the night with the music provided by violin and guitar. Although fancy clothing was rather difficult to acquire in isolated California, everyone was well dressed, according to Dana, and hopeful young *señoritas* sported elaborate floral corsages and carried bouquets to telegraph their present state of mind to would-be admirers. Mariano Chico, Colonial Governor of California at the time, ascribes the following meanings to the wearing of certain flowers at such events:

"Yerba Buena, I wish to be useful; Nasturtium, I wish to be a nun; Red rose, I am queen of my sex; White rose, I am queen of purity; Passion flower, hatred and rancor; Sunflower, I cannot bear the sight of you; Geranium, I will always love you; Hortensia, I wish to marry you; Gillyflower, I sigh for you; Violet, I am modest; Evergreens, my love is eternal." [6]

Lacking an excuse for some larger celebration, family and friends would often hold a *valecito casaro*, a kind of "at home" reception in the patio, usually to entertain house guests or for the purpose of announcing engagements. From all accounts, life in the balmy climate of pastoral California centered itself in the patio, under vine-covered *ramadas*, near the sounds of the well and the aromas of the oven. What little work the family engaged in was undertaken in the patio as well; sewing, preparing herbs for cooking and medicine, repairing clothing, or leatherwork of all kinds was undertaken in the patio area. Mundane tasks like washing, cooking, tending the animals, and all of the heavy work was done by the Indian cowboys (*vaqueros*) and farm hands (*gañanes*) for the rancho families.

A typical rancho patio of the California Pastoral Era. Nearly all of the plantings had practical as well as aesthetic value.

By the time of Dana's arrival on the California coast, improvements in carpentry, tools, and construction in general had greatly changed the quality and size of the California adobe house. By the 1830s, according to another early observer, Nellie Van de Grift Sanchez:

"A more luxurious mode of living was adopted, and some of the wealthier residents constructed commodious and even handsome houses after the Spanish tradition, built around an inner court filled with luxuriant plants watered by a fountain in the center. All around the court ran a corridor, upon which opened the large, dimly lighted rooms, with low ceilings, furnished sparsely, after the manner of the abstemious Spaniard. Here in peaceful California, grated windows were quite common, a relic from a day and place where a man's house had in reality to be his castle. The houses were usually of one story, never more than two. They had a look of solidity and permanency rather unusual in a new, frontier land." [7]

Mexico's independence from Spain in 1821 marked the end of the mission system's reign in California, and by 1834, the secularization of mission property was nearly complete—the padres having

returned to Spain, the Indians being released to wander. Soon thereafter, the mission buildings began to fall into ruin, some serving to provide materials for the enlargement of neighboring ranchos. If not removed, the roof timbers often rotted or split, giving way under the weight of heavy roof tiles, or they were carted away by scavenging *rancheros* and newly arriving American settlers. The adobe walls, now unprotected by broad overhangs, melted in the rain, returning to the soil from which they had been formed.

In some instances, mission gardens managed to fare better. One contemporary observer, William Robert Garner, noted in his journal on November 12, 1846:

"There are 21 missions in Upper California, and each of them have one or two large orchards, consisting of from 4 to 10 acres of land. All of these orchards are full of fruit trees, of different kinds and classes, and notwithstanding they have had no care taken of them for the last 6 or 8 years, still they yield fruit in abundance, and to my certain knowledge not one of these fruit trees have been pruned or attended to in any manner whatsoever for the space of 10 years. Besides the orchards, which contain apples, and pears of various kinds, peaches, pome-granates, plums, nectarines, and in the southern part of the territory, oranges in abundance. They have each, with the exception of two missions, one or two large vineyards which produce both the blue grape and the Muscatel in the highest perfection." [8]

Garner was an English adventurer who came to California in 1824 and served for a time as secretary to Walter Colton, the American *alcalde* in Monterey. His observations of the type of trees and conditions of the orchards are, doubtless, taken from observations of missions of the central coast. Therefore, they are unlikely to be accurate for San Gabriel, San Fernando, San Luis Rey and other southern missions where the interruption of irrigation had far greater effects. Garner's entry to his journal on November 25 noted: "Several of the old houses...were pulled down this year for the purpose of getting the timber they contained, which was redwood, and the beams and lintels were as sound, to all appearances, as the day they were put into those houses, which must have been some 60 to 70 years ago." [9]

It is an interesting testament to the quality of redwood truss roofs, which survive to this day, while the flat roofs made of local southern wood began to collapse within decades of their abandonment. More important perhaps, as suggested by Garner's journal, the gardens of the missions may well have been the single most significant legacy left to us from that era—to which our vast citrus, nut, and wine industries today attest.

Opposite: Ruins of the original adobe walls at Mission Nuestra Señora de la Soledad. Restoration of the chapel was begun in 1954 but remains largely unfinished. Above: Wild iris and poppy.

Following independence from Spain, the government in Mexico City began making generous grants on former mission lands, encouraging population growth in California, despite the fact that such lands, according to Spanish law, should have reverted to the Indians that continued to live there. Sadly, through trickery, theft or outright force, the Indians lost all legal title to the old mission lands, including the vast gardens and farmlands which the padres had left in trust to them. After some sixty years of subservience, the Indians no longer possessed the skills necessary for a return to their old hunter-gatherer life, nor could they compete in the world imposed on them. In addition to the bewildering changes in order and values, the Spanish also brought to California diseases for which the Indians had no natural immunity, and in the period between 1769 to 1821, the indigenous population of the colony shrunk from perhaps 300,000 to less than 50,000. Those Indian tribes who had lived under mission authority now found themselves to be the new servant class of the rapidly growing number of *ranchero* families.

For these new landowners, life in Mexican California was a time of easy living—large families, little work, and a simple economy based on tallow and hides. The cattle and horses that had first been driven north along the Anza Trail reproduced in staggering numbers in the mild, grassy valleys. With little real work to do, an agreeable year-round climate, and few problems to interfere with such pleasant occupations as riding, entertaining, and organizing an occasional *matanza* (slaughter and skinning), the *don* led a life of ease. According to contemporary accounts of pastoral life in California, a typical household might include as many as twenty servants to handle various chores: three or four to make the daily tortillas and do general kitchen work, five or six to do the washing for the family, the same number to spin the yarn and do some of the sewing, and usually a personal servant for each member of the household.

The houses of the traders and merchants of Monterey were somewhat different from those of the *rancheros*. As one might expect, refinements of all kinds could be found in the adobe dwellings of townspeople including plastered walls, wood floors and doors, and iron hinges and latches. Patios were enclosed by walls, separating neighbors and giving privacy from the street. Today, in many villages and colonial towns of Mexico, one can still experience the sense of order and the transition between spaces that was characteristic of such houses, beginning with an inviting gate at the street, leading through a high wall into a shaded patio with its central well and colorful plants in clay pots arranged to direct one towards the doorway of the house, another transi-

tion, and beyond this, perhaps another garden. Richard Henry Dana described the houses in Monterey during his visit there during 1835 and 1836:

"The town lay directly before us, making a very pretty appearance; its houses being plastered, which gives a much better effect than those of Santa Barbara, which are of mud color. The red tiles, too, on the roofs, contrasted well with the white plastered sides, and with the extreme greenness of the lawns upon which the houses—about a hundred in number—were dotted about, here and there, irregularly. Here and there a small patch is fenced in for a garden, so that houses are placed at random upon the green, which as they are of one story and of the cottage form, gives them a pretty effect when seen from a distance." [10]

Above: Patio of Mission San Carlos Borromeo de Carmelo, established by Junípero Serra in 1770, originally in Monterey and later in Carmel, as the headquarters of the mission chain.

Dana's fences refer to enclosures of vegetable patches, not patios, and the "greenness of lawns" reminds us that his visit to Monterey was during the rainy season. His appreciation for tile roofs and white plastered walls echoes through California's history even to the proliferation of mini-malls of the 1990s. Two other things in description of the houses, seen from anchor in the bay, point to improvements in local construction methods. Sometime around 1817 pitched roofs with redwood shingles had begun to replace the leaky, flat roof of tule reed and tar, and within another few years kiln-fired tiles, molded into half-cylinder shape for strength and lightness, had made their appearance, as Dana observed. Roof tiles of this material and form continued to be used in the construction of California houses until being replaced in the 1960s by a concrete imitation. The addition of plaster made with limestone, clay, mesquite ash, and the juice of the agave, rendered a tidy whiteness to Monterey houses, while window glass, wooden floors, and interior fireplaces were by this time fairly common in Monterey.

From the woman's perspective, we have Jane McDougal's observations of Monterey recorded in her journal while aboard the new steamship *California* on May 2, 1849—just thirteen years after Dana's visit:

"It is one of the most beautiful situations I ever saw on the sides of several hills which sloping back from the bay are partially covered with dark pines and partly with nothing but green grass. It has the appearance of beautiful green meadows or rolling prairies. It is certainly a lovely place at this season of the year, but I am told it is all parched up later in the year." [10a]

Tirey Ford, an early twentieth century resident, describes the Monterey house of 1830 as follows:

"Each householder built his house where his fancy dictated. If it happened to obstruct a bridle-path, no one questioned; simply went round. So the narrow thoroughfares zigzagged, in keeping with the carefree attitudes of the inhabitants. The buildings were mostly adobe, painted white and roofed with red tiles. There was plenty of adobe soil close at hand, from which the Indians could make bricks, grinding the lumps of clay in crude wooden mills, named *arastras*; treading it to a proper consistency with bare feet, mixing it with cut straw to give it tenacity, then drying the hand formed bricks in the sun. Timbers of joists, cross beams and rafters were hewn and shaped by hand from redwood, mostly, and the planks for floors and roof boards were split with wedges from the straight grained logs of the same great trees, growing in nearby canyons along the coast. Finally the whole building was plastered, inside and out, to give it finish and additional protection against the weather." [11]

Few of Monterey's old adobe buildings exist today; those remaining have suffered a variety of alterations from latter-day owners and occupants who valued comfort and convenience over historic significance. Thomas Larkin's house is an example. Built in 1835, possibly the first two-story adobe in town, its overhanging veranda, which helped to protect the wall below against sun and rain, was quickly copied and became an architectural fixture in Monterey. Larkin, a Boston merchant, had come to try his luck in California, and stayed to become the first, and only, United States consul to California. Across the street from the Larkin house stands the Cooper-Molera house, which was built in 1830 and is now fully restored, complete with herb and cutting gardens, corn rows, a grape arbor orchard of fruit trees, baking oven in the cluttered patio, and even the same species of poultry hens that ranged freely through the property in John Cooper's day. It is of passing interest to note that corn (*maize*), although introduced to European settlers by the American Indians, was unknown in California until the arrival of the padres, where it was planted in the mission gardens (*milpas*), as well as at Cooper's property. The potato arrived in Monterey from Peru by way of trading vessels looking for hides.

Most Monterey patios of this pastoral era were places of work and play alike, large enough to accommodate a small *huerta* (vegetable garden) and even a few sheep and goats in some cases.

Above: Charles Lummis' home, Los Angeles. Water-conserving garden restored in 1990 by Bob Perry.

5 5

But they could also be very pleasant, restful places, and were certainly the center of family life. Here is Ford's description of a Monterey patio of 1830:

"The patio was a sun flooded enclosure, gay with flowers and filled with palms, blossoming trees and ornamental shrubs. Giant ferns, sweet Castilian roses and fragrant jasmine framed nooks and fairy bowers. In the center was a sparkling fountain, the drops as they reached the sun, falling back in rainbow bubbles upon lily pads and the moss colored water in the stone basin below while the spray wafted a sense of delicious coolness. The garden beds were filled with flowers whose seed was brought from old Mexico; roses, pinks, hollyhocks, sweetpeas and orange lilies. No garden was considered complete without some form of cactus, usually a sharp-thorned century plant, with a stiff flowered stalk towering up into the blue, a straight, unbending sentinel guarding the plant world at its feet. Birds unmolested built their nests in the heavy, rose laden vines; white and yellow butterflies fluttered among Spanish bayonets. It was in the patio that the sun lingered longest, making the life within drowsy with its brightness." [12]

Ford, no doubt, takes some liberty with his picturesque description, and it must be remembered that the sun would be more welcome in Monterey, where a cool, moist climate prevails for much of the year. In sun-drenched Los Angeles, however, the patios were likely to be protected to some extent by shade trees and *ramadas*.

The original patio gardens of Old California, from Monterey to San Diego, have long disappeared—replaced more or less in accordance with contemporary taste, as well as by new arrivals from over the mountains who neither understood nor respected the ways of the pastoral era. Concerning the patio gardens of southern California, Victoria Padilla writes:

"There is unfortunately no authority in which to find a definite description of the gardens and their contents. Such information has been pieced together from stories handed down, from old diaries, letters, and accounts of visitors and from the remains of gardens that have survived the years." [13]

Bess Adams Garner is one of those who perused the old diaries and listened to the stories handed down from the old days. Her book, *Windows In An Old Adobe*, is a collection of the tales told to her by the great grandchildren of the original owners of Rancho San Jose, the Palomares and Vejar families. The ranch house was built in 1854 on a 15,000-acre Mexican land grant that today covers Pomona and adjoining areas. Garner's description of rancho life in southern California follows the daily routine of Doña Concepción ("China") Palomares:

Opposite: Corredor of the Palomares Adobe (Rancho San Jose), Pomona, was re-built in 1854, and restored from ruins in 1939-40.

"Doña China began to cut slips from her rose and geranium and lemon verbena bushes. The sheltered *corredor* along the north side of the house was crowded with growing things...rue, and costmary, poleo and marjoram. Gently Doña China persuaded a *capulin* cherry to grow...she would need some more slips of *Rosa de Castilla*...she would still need to toast rose petals over the fire and grind them in the tiny *metate* she kept for such things. Many chafed and fretting infants would still thank her for the rose dusting powder. She would need *rue* for earaches and asthma and *boraja* (thyme) for coughs, lemon verbena for tea...*poleo* (pennyroyal) and sage and spearmint and winter savory, marjoram, costmary and tarragon for seasoning. Her Indian women had taught her the use of *yerba santa* for coughs, probably it would be well, as she gathered castor beans from the clump in the garden, to have a few of them to plant...and she must have four o'clocks, not only for tea but for beads." [14]

The patio of a typical southern California home would also have the citrus fruit trees already mentioned, some shade trees such as the California pepper (actually native to tropical America and first brought to Mission San Luis Rey, near Oceanside, by Mexican sailors in 1830), and a *ramada* covered by night-blooming jasmine or grapevine.

The patio was the living room enclosed on three sides by a wall, arcade, or the covered *corredor*. The floor of the patio itself was tamped earth, although unglazed tile gradually came into greater usage, especially around the base of the centrally located well or fountain, and other areas of heavier foot traffic.

Herbs, annuals, and a variety of flowering and medicinal plants were usually grown in clay pots in the patio or planted along the base of the adobe walls or *corredor*. If there was a kitchen garden in the patio, it would include an area for growing cut flowers, as well as the herbs needed for flavoring.

Most of the restored adobes from the Spanish and Mexican eras have been encumbered with historically inaccurate gardens, consisting for the most part of neatly maintained lawns and a mixture of exotic plants from around the

world—none of which would likely have been found in Doña China's garden. When the Palomares adobe was restored on its one hundredth anniversary in 1940, there was also an effort made to reproduce the grounds in their original form. Today, Rancho San Jose displays a *ramada* covered in wisteria, a kitchen garden with a baking oven, an herb garden, native wildflowers and shrubbery, including California poppy, lupine, sage, agave, and roses.

A growing interest in California's history has produced a few more accurately restored patios and gardens of the pastoral era, such as the Hugo Reid adobe. Built in Arcadia, 1838, it is located on what is now a part of the Los Angeles County Arboretum. The Antonio Estudillo house, built in 1827 and located in Old Town, San Diego, is a far more sumptuous rancho. Abandoned in 1846, it was saved

from total destruction in 1905 by John D. Spreckles and is now a part of the San Diego Historic Park. One of the best restored of all the old adobes, it is unfortunate that the patio and gardens were not accorded similar concern.

Perhaps the largest of the old adobes is the ranch of General Mariano Vallejo, near Petaluma. Managed now by the State Department of Recreation and Parks, this large two-story structure has been carefully restored to reflect its 1834 appearance, complete with furnishings, baking oven, and ranching equipment typical of the period. Cattle munch the grass nearby as they might have done 150 years ago, and hides from a recent matanza dry in the sun on rough-sawn wood rails. Unfortunately, only half of the adobe has been rebuilt leav-

ing the interior patio exposed and unadorned. The department was also responsible for the restoration of La Purisima mission, near Lompoc. It is the only restoration that accurately portrays mission life in Spanish California.

Above: Patio of the Estudillo adobe, built in 1827 near the historic center of San Diego, and saved from ruin and destruction by John D. Spreckles in 1905. An accurate restoration of the patio itself remains to be done. Opposite: Exterior view of Estudillo Adobe.

Mariano Vallejo was the last commandant of military forces in northern California during the years of Mexican rule. His army was too small and poorly equipped to deal with either the threat of invasion by United States forces or the various moves towards independence for California by local agitators.

By 1840, Americans were becoming a familiar sight along the central coast, as well as the fertile inland valleys. Settlers, trappers, and adventurers like Jedidiah Smith and John Bidwell were making their way over the Rockies and the Sierra Nevada in increasing numbers in the 1840s. Trading ships from New England were becoming regular visitors to the growing California ports of San Diego, Santa Barbara, San Pedro, Monterey, and San Francisco, picking up hides and tallow in exchange for all manner of finished goods. Indeed, the

cattle business had made the *Californios* wealthy, just as their isolation from the Spanish and later Mexican governments had made them independent-minded. For years, these hospitable people welcomed the growing number of incoming Yankees with warmth and acceptance— to which both Hugo Reid and John Rogers Cooper could attest, both married locally and went on to become wealthy landowners and citizens in their adopted country.

Not all newcomers from the United States, however, made efforts to fit into the slow-paced easy going lifestyle of the *Californios*. Guadalupe Vallejo, nephew of the general, noted:

"The missions had avenues of fig, olive and other trees about the buildings, besides the orchards. In later times the American squatters often cut down these trees for firewood or

built fires against the trunks which killed them. Several hundred large olive trees at the San Diego mission were killed this way. The old orchards were pruned and cultivated with much care, but after sequestration of the mission property, they were neglected and ran wild. The olive mills and wine presses were destroyed and cattle were pastured in once fruitful orchards." [15]

A number of contemporary writers, as well as diarists, have described the wealth and variety of trees they found in California. In his journal for November 25, 1846, William Robert Garner wrote:

"There are several kinds of oaks in California, the large black oak is plentiful...about twelve miles south of Monterey there is a large cypress grove...Buttonwood, willow, poplar, alder, cottonwood and ash are very abundant all over the country, and some of these grow to immense size."[16]

The great British naturalist Thomas Nuttall, whom Richard Henry Dana befriended after meeting him on a southern California beach, also commented favorably on the variety and size of local trees, noting that buttonwood (California sycamore) was being used commonly in furniture-making in California. On the subject of buttonwood, or *aliso*, the younger Vallejo made this bitter notation in his diary:

"At the Mission San Jose there is a small creek and two very large sycamores once grew at the Spanish Ford, so that it was called El Aliso. A squatter named Fallon cut down these for firewood, though there were many trees in the canyon. The Spanish people begged him to leave them, for shade and beauty, but he did not care for that." [17]

Despite the variety described by early chronologers, the lack of trees was a significant hardship for both Mexican and American settlers in the 1840s. In southern California, the coast live oak was nearly the only construction-grade wood available for roof timbers and other structural uses. As more Americans arrived, the competition for lumber, as well as the destructive salvaging from mission buildings, greatly increased.

Below: Mission La Purisima Concepcion, near Lompoc, was restored from 1935-1941, as a State Historic Park, and is today the most complete mission complex in the system. Opposite: Carreta, restored Cooper-Molera garden, Monterey.

American California

United States troops invaded California from both north and south in 1846. There was, for a short time, some sentiment for independence fostered by *Californio* and American settlers alike, but this quickly evaporated with the successful campaigns of John C. Fremont in Sonoma and Stephen W. Kearny across the south to San Diego and Los Angeles. Monterey was seized in July, 1846, by Commodore John Sloat, virtually ending Mexico's rule, as well as any lingering hope for an independent California.

With the Treaty of Guadalupe Hidalgo, signed near Mexico City in May, 1848, California began to lose its pastoral, easy lifestyle, and with the discovery of gold in 1849 at John Sutter's sawmill on the American River near Coloma, rapid changes in the economic and demographic character of the state occurred. The Yankee settlers who followed the trail of gold, accustomed as they were to the green meadows and woodlands of their eastern river valleys, were not so accepting of the arid, rugged landscape they had come to conquer and claim. As the population of San Francisco and surroundings began to swell from gold fever, the new arrivals from Boston and St. Louis alike ignored the sensible adobe construction and cut down the local oak, sycamore, pine, cypress, and redwood to build houses like those they had left behind.

They also rejected the enclosed patio, with its life-giving well, tamped earth floor, fruit trees, and climbing roses, in favor of imported turfgrass, front porches, and bedding gardens facing the street—a usefulness entirely aesthetic. For most of the latter half of the nineteenth century, California gardens would

reflect eastern American taste and style. Just as Carpenter Gothic—a western version of Victorian architecture rendered in wood—replaced the simplicity of the tile-roofed adobe, flower gardens, foundation planting, bedding rows, and other forms of lineal gardens replaced the spatial, enclosed, and functional garden of the Spanish and Mexican eras.

Near the beginning of the twentieth century, Californians began to restore the ruined missions and many of the old adobes, and this important historic work continues to this day. One of the oldest existing adobes, El Molino Viejo, built in 1816 in San Marino, was restored in part during the 1920s with only a few old photographs and sketchy written accounts for guidance.

Above: El Molino Viejo in San Marino, started about 1816 (a grinding mill up to the American era) and restored over many years during the 1920s and 1930s. Today, it is a landmark adobe building and local headquarters for the California Historical Society. Photo, 1936.
Opposite: Patio of the Molino Viejo

Another important restoration, the Guajome Adobe, is more recent. Once the home of a Yankee emigre named Cave Couts (who stripped lumber and other materials from nearby Mission San Luis Rey), this large two-story adobe was built in 1853 in San Diego County during the waning years of the pastoral era. Helen Hunt Jackson stayed at Guajome while gathering material for her novel, *Ramona*, a dramatization of which is performed annually near Hemet.

Complete reconstructions of adobes, when they are historically accurate, are also worth noting. In Los Angeles, the Casa de Adobe on Figueroa Street near the Southwest Museum is a reasonable replica of a pastoral era house. Built by the Hispanic Society in 1917, it contains period furnishings and materials. But the most interesting aspect is its patio garden, which is planted in accordance with written descriptions from period letters and documents. Growing there today are the plants of a typical 1840s patio: rue (used in medicine and food preparation), lemon verbena (for flavoring and aroma), lavender (flowers used in sachets and perfumes), mint (for flavoring), sage (both native and Mediterranean for medicines and cooking), jasmine (for aroma), thyme (for flavoring and cooking), and Castilian rose (for talcum and perfumes). Annuals brought from Mexico may also be found growing in the garden, as well as grapes from those originally brought to Mission San Gabriel sometime after its founding in 1771. Trees in the patio include California bay (whose leaves are used in cooking), pomegranate, orange, fig, and datura. Mexicana dahlias, favored for their purplish-blue flowers, grow here as well.

The Casa de Adobe, although only a replica of an Old California patio, serves today to remind us of the charm of the simple pastoral-age garden. A worthwhile project for California's gardeners and history buffs in consort would be the accurate restoration of patio gardens at remaining adobe houses and ranchos. Enclosure, variety of usage, and water-conserving plantings are becoming as important to Californians today as they were two hundred years ago.

Top: Casa de Adobe, Los Angeles, a reconstruction in 1917 of a traditional Old California adobe ranch house. It remains a center for domestic history.

Middle: Padre flower.

Opposite: Gated entrance to a private courtyard.

III.

Mediterranean Revival

'And if I kiss you in the garden,
In the moonlight, will you pardon me,
Come tiptoe through the tulips with me.'

Joe Burke, Al Dubin
Tiptoe Through The Tulips, 1924

Opposite: Arthur Zwebell's Los Angeles area
courtyard garden—Villa d'Este—this 1920s courtyard
garden was intended to provide residents with a
sense of Andalusian intimacy.

During the first fifty years of statehood, California seemed to shrink from its Hispanic roots in favor of the eastern vogue for large wood and brick houses fronted by conspicuous splashes of floral decoration, colorful shrubbery from Asia and the tropics, and broad terraces of green turf glistening in the benign sunlight. But towards the end of the century, the Golden State was once again turning to Spain—and to the Mediterranean world generally—for both architectural and garden inspiration.

A number of different names identify this cultural swing, including: pastoral revival, mission revival, Spanish colonial revival. None, however, accurately describes what was really happening, particularly in respect to the word, 're-vival.' True, a renewed interest in the old missions had begun to surface around 1900, leading to a peculiar array of restoration programs, some accurate, some wildly off-mark. For example, in Santa Clara the replica mission is part of the university, complete with classes, and the Santa Cruz mission was re-built at a Disney-like half scale. The gardens, for the most part, were never restored, and the cloisters and patios were re-planted to reflect the taste of the restoration era itself. Re-building of some of the old ranchos also occurred. But this renewed interest in revival during the early 1900s came not so much from the romantic ruins of old missions and adobes—the impact of *Ramona* notwithstanding—but from a fascination with the Mediterranean world itself, particularly with Spain and Italy.

Opposite: "Patio Party" by Deloyht-Arendt (47103 386-160), courtesy Romm Art Creations, Glen Cove, NY.

There were of course the natural similarities—long arid summers, mild, moist winters—that identify the Mediterranean climate the world over. But changing fashion, particularly a growing interest in European taste, directed Californians away from the fusty, flowery Victorian style of garden design, in style since the gold rush days, and toward a more sedate, hard-edged version of Spanish, Italian, and even Islamic garden design.

During the half-century following statehood, California embarked on a frenzied rush of commercial and industrial growth that swept away nearly all remaining traces of the old pastoral way of life. Railroads and boat canals were soon speeding merchandise and farm produce towards the population centers of the midwest and east coast. Within a few decades of joining the United States, California emerged as an industrial giant in its own right, with more than its share of wealthy entrepreneurs, shipping and lumber magnates, and real estate tycoons. Adding to this growing economic clout came the motion picture industry, which created an Arabian Nights aura of glistening beaches and waving palms, of flying carpets, canopied oases, Persian gardens, and silvery moonscapes.

With the rail connection made between San Francisco and Los Angeles in 1876, southern California began to grow, and by the turn of the century, thanks largely to the completion of the Southern Pacific Railroad, Los Angeles began to rival San Francisco, Sacramento, and the other northern towns. Agriculture, particularly the citrus industry, and motion pictures provided much of the economic clout, and soon the newly prosperous were busily building the palaces of their dreams in Pasadena, Beverly Hills, Bel Air, Santa Barbara, and Montecito—palaces that ri-

valed their counterparts in Tuscany, Andalusia, or even Xanadu. For inspiration it was, of course, necessary to travel to such places personally, to fully understand and appreciate the centuries-old stately homes and gardens, and with a rather sudden surge in steamer bookings, the era of the "Grand Tour" was launched. Wealthy Californians returned from their Mediterranean sojourns eager to duplicate the grandeur they had observed in places like Spain's Alhambra and Italy's Villa d'Este, determined to create something similar of their own.

Left: Step details of Mediterranean revival gardens in Pasadena.

Opposite: Arid landscape of Andalusia, with olive trees.

Below: Jefferson estate in Montecito, Paul Thiene, landscape architect.

The craze for all things Mediterranean was further stimulated in 1915 by the simultaneous openings of two California world's fairs—the Panama-Pacific Exposition in San Francisco and the Panama-California Exposition in San Diego, both celebrating the completion of the Panama Canal. The San Francisco fair had greater status and backing, including the official sanction of the federal government and such noteworthy designers as architect Bernard Maybeck and Golden Gate planner John McLaren. But it was the upstart San Diego fair, built in previously undeveloped Balboa Park, that proved to have the greater impact on public taste, spreading churrigueresque (after Jose Churriguera, eighteenth century Spanish architect) volutes and arabesques across southern California. Particularly remarkable in their ornate detailing were the opulent new motion picture theatres and gasoline service stations—two southern California institutions almost from the outset.

Above: The Panama-California Exposition, Balboa Park, San Diego, 1915. Tropical plant importation developed rapidly in southern California at this time.

Opposite: Detail of principal garden pool and spray fountain, the Generalife.

Save for Maybeck's rotunda and the surrounding grounds, virtually nothing remains of San Francisco's elaborately formal fair, but San Diego's exposition was so well received that most of the buildings, grounds, and gardens were retained and improved to serve as a future world's fair location, as well as for regular park usage to this day. Bertram Goodhue was the overall coordinating architect, with Paul Thiene and Kate Sessions involved in planning the grounds.

Whether inspired by the expositions, the "Grand Tour", the films of Rudolph Valentino, the similarity of climate, or some lingering longing for an historic legacy, California, by 1920, had thoroughly immersed itself in Mediterranean and Persian eclecticism. But whenever suitable, the emphasis was Spanish. Department stores, public schools, state office buildings and grounds, the substations of the Metropolitan Water District, apartment complexes with names like 'The Garden of Allah', and even industrial plants began to assume the trappings of Moorish and Hispanic idiom. Mail-order bungalow plans were converted from Craftsman to Spanish, and tile manufacturers could not keep up with demand for the brightly glazed geometric patterns that framed every fireplace, every kitchen window, lintel, and wall niche.

But nowhere was this fascination more keenly observed than in the art of garden design. The Mediterranean garden, popular throughout much of United States in the 1920s, was almost obligatory in California. In planning their gardens, the Franciscan padres and Spanish settlers of the late eighteenth century had only their memories of Andalusia, few materials, and the help of Indian laborers to carry out a design. Wealthy Californians of the 1900s could, however, visit the gardens of Spain, as well as the Persian and Italian Renaissance gardens of Rome, Tuscany, and Lombardy. They would return to California from Spain with photographs of Granada's Alhambra gardens to show their architects and landscape architects what they wanted for their own hillside overlooking Silver Lake or the Pacific Ocean. Promoting their use in California, Helen Morganthau Fox wrote glowingly in the early 1920s of the beauty and propriety of traditional Spanish gardens:

> "They are a shaded green paradise, scented with frequent plants, cooled by rippling waters and secluded by vine-clad walls from the dusty world without. For Spain, like the Southwest, is a parched, brown country where the purple shadows stand out sharply in the glare of the fierce blue sky." [18]

Left: Interior patio at "Lotusland," used by Madame Ganna Walska during her tenure as owner. The landscape architect was Ralph Stevens, the son of the original owners.

Opposite: Garden of the Generalife, Alhambra, Granada, Spain

Roots
of the
Spanish
Garden

The gardens that Fox admires and describes so poetically in *Patio Gardens* were the result of a long history going back to North Africa and the Spain of the Caesars, back further to the Mesopotamian world of Assyria and Babylonia, and even before those mighty empires to earlier civilized communities created by Sumerians and Akkadians, earlier still, to the first recorded architectural remains of the Fertile Crescent, built nearly 10,000 years ago. Indeed, according to recent archaeological findings and their possible interpretations, somewhere on the marshy plain between the conflux of the Tigris and Euphrates Rivers where ancient irrigation systems first brought agriculture to the edges of the arid valleys, somewhere between the cities of Samarra in the north and Ur, near the Persian Gulf, lies the Garden of Eden itself—The Earthly Paradise.

From such beginnings, from such disparate, time-laden cultures that represent the evolution of the Spanish garden

Below: Restored fragment of the Canopus, Hadrian's villa, second century A.D., Tivoli (near Rome).

at the height of Moorish ascendancy, a few obvious similarities between these ancient societies occur, principally their low annual rainfall, high summer temperatures, and their lack of stone and wood. This led to imaginative use of clay in Mesopotamia, for everything from irrigation pipe to structural walls and plant containers—as found in artists' reconstructions of the famous, if mythical, Hanging Gardens. Here, in Mesopotamia, the rose was known to be first cultivated as early as 3000 B.C.

The earliest garden makers in Spain, the Romans, used stone and concrete, as well as brick for bearing walls, domes, and arches when stone was not readily available. Accustomed to the dry, hot climate of North Africa, the Romans built houses bearing thick walls of sundried brick and enclosed courtyards that served as places of work and leisure. Such courtyards, called atriums, were used for a variety of activities including growing herbs and food for the table, another for the collecting of rain water from the roof gutters, a third for family gathering and entertaining.

The conquering Visagoths of the fifth century were not much interested in preserving Roman courtyards, nor did they maintain the great aqueducts and water storing systems of the Romans. As a result, the gardens quickly with-

ered and the evolution of garden design stalled in Spain until the beginning of the eighth century, when the Arabic Moors commenced their slow and largely peaceful invasion of the Iberian Peninsula. They followed the old Roman route from North Africa across the Straits of Gibraltar, bringing to Europe their advanced mathematics and astronomy, their knowledge of irrigation, hydraulics and agriculture, their philosophy and literature, and their skills in engineering and architecture—as well as a love for garden making.

Above Left: Patio of the Palacio de Viana, Córdoba.

Above Right: Water stairway, The Alhambra.

After visiting the remnants of ancient Moorish gardens in Spain, British garden historians Mildred and Arthur Byne concluded:

"The true Spanish garden is of Asiatic derivation; it harks back to Persia during her splendor under the Sassanids—the garden the Arabs found when they conquered her. The Moors, who made gardens in Spain, were no artless children of nature. Their Moslem tradition was one of order, science, everything pre-arranged. A garden was not a walled-off piece of cultivated ground; it was a man-made design that permitted nature to play a small part, nothing more." [19]

The Moors were originally of Syrian Arabic descent (converts to Islam) who spread their new faith from Damascus westward across North Africa and eventually into Spain. From Syria they brought medicine and technical knowledge, and from nearby Persia they acquired their love for gardens and the plants cultivated there including orange, jasmine, pomegranate, rose.

Their irrigation technology, which was far in advance of Roman methods, was the key to making the many artificial oases that soon began to dot the Andalusian hillsides. Aided in their endeavors by immigrating Jews and Byzantine Greeks, these Moors went on to build the cities of Seville, Granada, and Córdoba, centers of civilization and learning in an otherwise Dark Age. Eventually the Moors and their allies occupied all but the northwestern part of Spain, where the newly formed Visigothic-Christian kingdoms of Castile, Leon, Navarre, and Aragon reigned. But it was Andalusia that best suited the Moors, and it was here in the south of Spain that they left their greatest monuments to architecture and garden

design: The Alcázar in Seville and the Medina Azahara in Córdoba. But little remains of these and other great Moorish gardens of Andalusia. Dependent upon the intricate water tapping, carrying, holding, and delivery systems designed by the Moorish engineers, that included valley-spanning stone aqueducts that reached into the Sierra Morena, stone-lined clay pipe laid underground, and huge reservoirs to maintain a water supply and con-

Above: Palacio de Viana, principal interior patio.

Opposite left: Courtyard of the shrine at Imamzadeh, Kashan, Iran.

Opposite right: Bagh-i-fin (courtyard garden), at 15th century Shah Abbas garden, Iran.

stant water pressure throughout the long dry season, the gardens quickly withered when these were neglected and destroyed by succeeding centuries of Berber and Christian resurgence. From the few that have been partially restored, the gardens of the Alhambra for instance, the heritage of the Spanish garden has been preserved.

In addition to the legacy left by the Romans and Moors, the gardens of Spain owe much to Islam itself and to earlier Persian influences. The Islamic religion was barely a century old when the Moors crossed the Straits of Gibraltar and entered Europe in 701, introducing their science, art, and philosophy to the region. The character of medieval Spain began to take on a distinctly Moorish quality during succeeding centuries, but it was the Islamic garden that came to symbolize the faith of the Prophet and to best illustrate Moorish technology. Indeed, science, art, and philosophy were combined to create the Islamic garden—an extension of paradise.

In Persia and India, as well as in Moorish Spain, the garden was structured in a tradition of geometric symmetry. This strict order to design was intended to symbolize moral ethics, as well as paradise on earth, employing a ground plan that was both centric and quadrilateral for the purpose of denoting the universality of being and place. The typical garden plan was thus focused centrally and divided into four equal sections, suggesting life, growth, death, and rebirth. Together, the cruciform plan represented eternity, perfect in its proportions, changing only with the seasons of life.

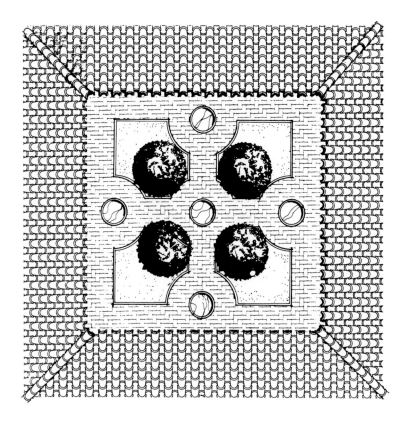

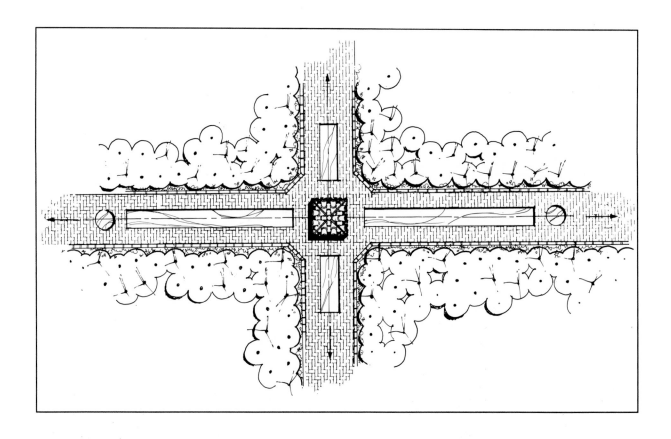

Water was of course the life blood of the Islamic garden, always in motion, yet at times appearing placid and reflective in shallow, rectangular pools, nurturing and sustaining both the spiritual and the tangible.

Plants in the Persian garden play their symbolic roles as well, representing stages of life and principles of conduct; the cypress being a symbol of eternity, continuity or death, the flowering almonds and plums representing birth, renewal and change. Plants were also selected for their aromas and their ability to attract singing birds into the garden.

That the garden was also intended for pleasure should be obvious to anyone familiar with Persian paintings, in which scenes of love-making, meditation, diverse recreational pursuits, and symbolic events are easily discernible in even the miniature compositions. In even more sensual terms, *The Perfumed Garden*, a fifteenth-century instructional book on carnal pleasure, weaves a fleshly, aromatic fabric; "Fill your tent with a variety of perfumes: amber, musk, all sorts of scents, as rose, orange flowers, jonquils, jessamine, hyacinth, carnation, and other plants." [20] Also favored in the Islamic garden were pistachio and almond for their nuts; red, yellow, and white roses; fruit trees such as peach, citrus, apricot, plum, and quince; a variety of grape vines, and, in addition to the cypress, such trees as oriental sycamore, willow, and poplar. In addition to the wild birds drawn to the garden in search of nectar, caged birds were present as well, chosen for colorful plumage and for their sweet songs. Bulbuls were particularly popular as were paddling ducks and swans.

Two distinctly different garden concepts emerged from these Islamic origins. The courtyard garden, which eventually became the Spanish patio garden, was centripetal (directed inward, toward the center), symmetrical, generally level or perhaps slightly lowered at the center, and marked by a visually arresting focal element at the center—usually a raised fountain. The second type, which developed primarily in Persia and India, is centrifugal (directed away from the center), following the principal and secondary axes outward towards termini at the garden edges. These Persian and Moghul gardens tend to be larger than the enclosed Moorish gardens of Spain, and at their center—the crossing of the axes—is usually found the garden pavilion, soul of the entire complex. Moghul gardens are exemplified by Shalimar in Kashmir and Hasht Bihisht in Isfahan, both of which have pavilions at the crux of their intersecting axes.

Both are similar in terms of their geometric, cruciform design, with emphasis on privacy and repose. This four-parted or quadrilateral lay-out, called *chuhar bagh*, symbolizes the four mystic rivers of Islam. In the Moorish garden, this may be represented by a central pool, square or circular, with four narrow channels leading from it. The Moghul garden would likely begin at the central pavilion, the highest point, and extend outward along the four axes over a series of descending levels formed by interconnected pools and gardens, eventually to finite elements acting as visual termini (see opposite page.)

Opposite: Typical Moghul garden (top), and Moorish garden (bottom).

Italian Influence

In a similar way, the Italian Renaissance garden of the sixteenth-century was organized along a principal sight-line (axis), always descending, falling through a series of connected levels called parterres and having any number of right-angle cross axes, usually located at points of vertical change where steps and retaining walls are called into usage.

The Villa Lante, designed by Giacomo da Vignola in 1564, is perhaps the finest example of both the quality of design and the artistic philosophy of the High Renaissance. Vignola was an established architect and rival to Michelangelo in and around Rome, but it was his sensitivity and skill in garden design that placed him at a level of singular esteem. At Lante, for example, he controls nature in a symbolic way, dividing the natural hillside into a series of measured levels and converting the natural flow of the stream and its inlets into a sharply defined watercourse, complete with waterfalls, fountains, pools, and cascades—a concert of visual performances, all of which suggest mankind's ability to harness the wild forces of nature. In his effort to demonstrate nature's obeisance, Vignola was careful to place architecture in a subordinate role. It is the garden alone which strikes us on entering the villa. The same reaction undoubtedly was felt by touring Californians in the early 1900s, and it was this seemingly magical quality that they hoped to replicate in their homes in Montecito and Bel

Air. Like Spain, Italy is subject to similar climatic conditions. Therefore, visiting Californias were impressed, not only by the year-round aspects of garden use, but also by a host of Italian plants including laurel, myrtle, broad-leafed evergreens, conifers, and, of course, the ubiquitous Italian cypress.

Thus, from the Renaissance world of Vignola, the Islamic world of Moghul, Persian, and Moorish gardens, the ancient Mesopotamian and Roman court-yards, and from the Franciscans and settlers of New Spain, the ancestry of the California Garden is joined.

While the chart (right) clarifies the lineage of the California garden up to the beginning of the twentieth-century, some confusion persists in efforts to identify a particular Mediterranean Revival garden's derivation.

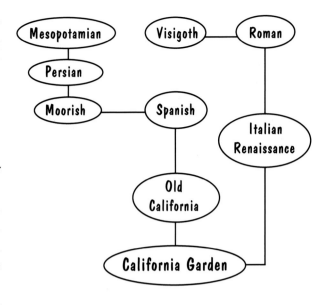

Opposite: Detail of garden steps, Villa Farnese, Caprarola, designed by Giacomo da Vignola in late sixteenth century. Below: Plan of the Villa Lante.

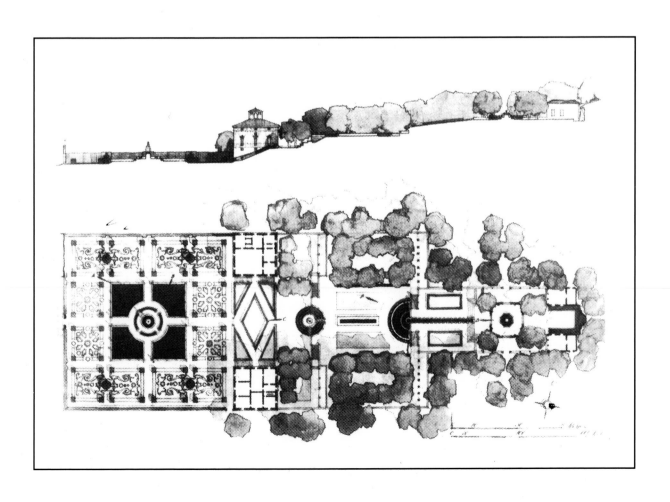

This is usually the result of the touring Californians' eclectic tastes and their willingness to borrow stylistic elements from a variety of architectural and garden forms observed on their travels. And while architects and landscape architects of the era seemed quite willing to apply the whims of their clients to whatever the prospect, it was often the designers themselves who became caught up in the crush to Hispanize or Italianize the hills of California. In some instances they copied entire gardens, house and all, but more often they simply borrowed what appealed to them— fountains, parterres, statuary—this *giardino segreto* (hidden garden), that *glorieta* (Spanish summer house). And in the smaller gardens, including the plethora of Spanish bungalows that began to line the streets of Alhambra, San Gabriel, El Monte, and Glendale, both Spanish and Italian details were reduced to easily reproduceable clichés: tile roof, lunette window, corkscrew column, wrought-iron gate and window grille, tiled stoop, and blue and green glazed tiles set into step risers. Mass produced plans often called for a Spanish quatre-foil fountain and a miniaturized version of the enclosed front patio together with pittosporum or eugenia hedges having globular corners and endings.

Top: Italianate cascade on garden side of "Las Tejas," (tiles, tiled roof), the Montecito estate of Oakleigh Thorne, as it looked in 1928. Garden by Mrs. Thorne.

Opposite: Gardens of the Alhambra

The Spanish Garden

Since Spain has played the major role in influencing California garden design, it is important to understand the purposes, form, materials, and character of the Spanish garden itself.

First of all, in keeping with Moorish precepts, it is a relatively small space, enclosed by surrounding architecture, a patio. The Alhambra, Granada's great Moorish castle, contains four principal patio gardens, the largest of which is only 120 feet long by 75 feet wide. Although the Spanish garden draws upon nature for symbolism and inspiration, natural form is not rendered in abstract, reductive terms as in an English or Japanese garden. Instead, the principles of balance, line, proportion, form, and color are applied to garden design as they would be to architecture. A Spanish garden is normally both geometric and centric (centrifugal), focused inward towards a fountain or pool. The design is uncluttered, simple and direct. Except for perhaps a service gate, entry into the garden is from inside the house. Entry gardens, with a gate opening from the street, follow much the same arrangement.

A Spanish garden is without grass, the floor being tamped earth, river gravel, crushed stone or compressed granite; it is divided geometrically by tiled pathways on either diagonal or right-angle axes that cross at the center. Sometimes rounded pebbles of various colors cemented into intricate patterns are combined with unglazed terra cotta tiles that trim and accent the patio floor. The hard edging that results is softened and aesthetically balanced by clay pots filled with seasonal perennials or flowering shrubs placed to direct traffic and emphasize sitting areas, as well as to line the base of fountains, pools, and the edges of stairways. Most pots are of a similar shape—cylindrical, slightly flared, and taller than their diameter to promote good root development and to reduce water needs. Made by hand, clay pots are often glazed in bright colors to contrast with the surrounding tile, gravel, or tamped earth. A Spanish house may also be built around a central patio, which has an interior entry to several different rooms and serves as a principal gathering place for the family. Interior patios are usually tiled completely, often in black and white, as well as earth colored glazing.

The design of the patio garden is primarily a matter of establishing a sense of space. This is usually achieved by enclosing walls and by making use of the facade of the house itself, which in any case acts as one or more of the garden walls. Enclosure may also be achieved by use of plants in the form of green walls or in vine-colored trellises and arbors to provide the garden with a leafy overhead, but always reflecting the geometry of the architecture and softening the transition from plastered ceiling to spacious Spanish sky.

There is also an attempt to achieve a sense of *place* with the patio acting as transition between house and the outdoor world. For example, the siting of the Alhambra allows for magnificent views from certain patios overlooking Granada and the surrounding countryside. Many California gardens of the 1920s, especially in and around west Los Angeles, were similarly sited to take advantage of views from the garden into canyons and reservoirs below.

The walls of a Spanish garden are made of clay block, not unlike our own adobe, and smoothly stuccoed or painted in chalky hues of ochre, creamy white, azure, salmon pink or pale aquamarine, and capped with glazed tile, usually a glossy blue or green. Sometimes the walls have windows that face the street with brightly painted wood shutters, louvered for privacy. There is usually a lacy wrought-iron grille as well and seats on either side of the window, built at right angles into the thick wall where *señoritas* might sit and watch quietly for likely suitors among the passing throng outside.

Vines such as bougainvillea, jasmine, passionflower, trumpet vine, or any of a long list of aromatic climbing roses may cover the interior side of the garden wall. Plant material is carefully selected for practical, as well as ornamental use, and orange, almond or pomegranate trees might be planted for shade and sustenance. Low hedges of box or myrtle accent geometric patterns while tall hedges of cypress and yew outline the garden's structure and serve as inner walls or separators between interior garden spaces. Older Moorish gardens offered little change in color beyond varying shades of green, but flowers of every kind dominated most of the gardens visited by touring Californians, then as today.

Opposite top: The patio home of architect Luta Marie Riggs, Montecito, about 1928.

Opposite bottom: The Dodge House, designed by Irving Gill in 1914, illustrates the architect's skill in blending traditional hispanic detail with a newly emerging modern form. Gardens remain principally Mediterranean. In Los Angeles, it has since been destroyed.

The most important element in the Spanish garden, however, is water. In the little pools and basins, it reflects the deep blue of the Andalusian sky or flows evenly over the smooth stone rim of bubbling fountains.

Water in the Andalusian garden, long before the introduction of recirculating pumps, was both a symbol and a fact of life. It played this dual role of providing pleasure, as well as sustenance, in an oasis-like setting. Distinctly Spanish are the narrow runnels, lined with blue or green glazed tiles, that carry trickling ribbons of water away from the central source and along the main axis, dropping again to a lower pool and continuing downward to fulfill its final garden role—irrigation. The enclosed garden, with its aroma of jasmine, its plump pomegranates and oranges, its soft murmur of water, becomes a cool and pleasant refuge from a harsh outside world. It was this quality, this image that the mission padres and the Spanish settlers hoped to bring, by way of Mexico, to California.

That such a place can be practical, as well as aesthetically and spiritually restful, becomes more evident when one visits a Spanish home today. The heavy old cypress gate is bolted against the traffic of the street, just the other side of a high, vine-clad wall. Water is drawn from a well for washing, some splashing over the tiles. Children play at various games, their voices in sharp contrast to the noises of the street. Odd jobs of repair are undertaken in the sunlit places where good light is needed, or in the shade of a tule-covered ramada on a hot summer afternoon. Just before the old bell announces *la cena*, a young girl comes into the patio from the kitchen and pokes a stick up into the branches of the tree shading a louvered window,

collecting in her apron the limes that fall to the hard earthen surface below. A handful of roses are clipped and placed in a little vase of water in the center of the table.

Opposite: Detail of the Alcázar gardens, Córdoba

Above: This garden and cascade, reminiscent of the Italian Renaissance, is located in Lafayette park, Los Angeles, and was originally owned by film actress Deanna Durbin.

The Spanish garden impresses us with its emphasis on privacy and function, qualities shared to some degree in Italy and France as well. Californians, with this Mediterranean heritage, understand these values to a far greater degree than do most other Americans. Indeed, when the Yankees began to invade California in large numbers, bringing with them their midwestern garden ethic, they were suspicious of the enclosed patio, favoring their familiar sweep of lawn, flower bed, and front porch—the customary trappings of the American garden. It is still one of the cultural differences which separate northern and southern Europe from American and northern European garden concepts to this day. In 1981, Rene Dubos, the celebrated French environmentalist, touched on it while comparing contrasts between French and American gardens:

"To my taste, the American garden is almost objectionably public. I cannot imagine any more glaring contrast as a background to social relationships than the enclosed intimate foyers and gardens hidden behind the dull but protective walls of French streets, and the picture windows and lawns opened to the public eye which are almost the rule in American settlements." [21]

Rule indeed. In almost every American community, frontyard setbacks are dictated by law, which also invariably prescribes minimum levels of planting and maintenance. Front fencing and walls are restricted as well, usually to no more than three feet in height, and while city ordinances are more relaxed in regard to hedges and plant screens, the intent, as Dubos observes, is to provide the passerby with an open view of your property—to your very front door. In California, such regulations exist as well, but are more readily relaxed, one believes, when addressed by a carefully conceived landscape plan.

Although California garden design was greatly influenced during the early twentieth century by southern Europe and Mediterranean ideas in particular, there were many individuals, artists, architects, and historians who preferred a return to pastoral California for inspiration: One of these was architect Rexford Newcomb, who made this plea in 1924:

"Those who have strolled through the cloisters of the old missions or have sketched in the patios of the old houses know the charm and appropriateness of these interesting old folk expressions, crude and unrefined as they may appear in the light of our own day. That they were honest, straight-forward and sincere—quali-

ties unfortunately not characteristic of a great deal of our own modern work—also cannot be denied. What then should the designers of today, with improved materials and good craftsmen, not be able to produce? The cue of honest craftsmanship is offered to him. Let him take it, and having mastered the abiding principles of the style, turn to his modern problems and seek to express the life and tenor of our own times in the spirit of the Spanish Colonial, one of the few architectures appropriate to a land with the climate of California, and the Hispanic background she possesses." [22]

Newcomb, like Helen Morganthau Fox, hoped to encourage a Spanish colonial revival in California, more in the line of the state's historic roots than climatic similarities with Mediterranean countries. But the memories of gray frocked friars, Indian neophytes, Spanish *presidios, vaqueros and rancheros*—no matter how madly they were remembered to have danced their *fandangos* and galloped their dusty trails—were not in themselves sufficient to overcome the elaborate desires of the Golden State's new gentry—real estate tycoons, land promoters, rail and shipping barons, movie makers—and their architects. Newcomb feared that a Mediterranean revival was more of a reflection of Renaissance Europe than Old California, and of course this was the case.

Left: Base of birdbath at "Lotusland," in pebble mosaic.

Opposite: Casa del Herrero, Montecito, 1925-28. Reverse view looking back toward house, on axis. Ralph Stevens, landscape architect.

As the Mediterranean revival in California progressed, the make-believe world of film seemed to grow and develop alongside, not so very different from the real world that the motion picture people were creating for themselves. Rudolph Valentino *became* The Sheik, Douglas Fairbanks *became* Zorro, and Harold Lloyd built a mansion on a hilltop above Beverly Hills and filled it with a series of gardens that would have rivaled those of any pasha or Renaissance Cardinal. Life in movieland had taken to imitating art—the celluloid sand of the soundstage commingling with the real palms and beaches. Only a sultan's garden would do for the new dream merchants, encouraged, no doubt, by such extravagantly romantic products as *The Desert Song*, with these 1926 lyrics:

"If one flower grows

alone in your garden,

Soft petals blooming, will

wither away,

But bowers should be

overflowing,

With sweet passion

flowers of varied

perfume." [23]

This blurring of reality and romance is further revealed in Winifred Dobyns' otherwise straightforward descriptions of California's newly created Mediterranean gardens:

"Plants have been brought here from every quarter of the globe and they thrive happily together in their adopted country...water lies in reflecting pools which mirror mountain vistas...it mur-

murs down bright tile runnels in garden paths, to fall into gay pools of Spanish and Moorish prototypes...there is much of magic in these California gardens. Perhaps it is the quality of light which bathes them in sun or moon shine." [24]

It is interesting to recall that Helen Morganthau Fox urged Californians to create Spanish-styled gardens in the late 1920s, then to discover that suggestion brought to reality only two or three years later in Winifred Dobyns' album of California gardens of the era. Everyone it seems was in a hurry to proclaim the latest Hispanic, Italian, or Persian garden in southern California, and the hillsides above west Los Angeles, Pasadena, Santa Barbara, and Montecito were becoming sprinkled with the mansions of the wealthy, and their Mediterranean gardens of brick-edged regularity—lineal, axial, hard-surfaced and geometric. Dobyns was one of the first to describe these gardens in spatial terms:

"Outdoor living rooms are a most important element in California gardens. These may take the form of a cloistered patio, almost a part of the house itself, with overshadowing olive trees and murmuring fountains, or of a flagged sitting area beneath the spread of a majestic live oak." [25]

Top: Mack Sennet silent film starlets posing with sweetpeas. A publicity booster for southern California in the late 1920s.

Bottom: Los Angeles Chamber of Commerce publicity photo intended to stimulate interest in southern California. 1931.

How far did Californians go in the pursuit of Mediterranean themes? The Alhambra's gardens were too formal surely, both in use and design, for California living of 1920. The elaborate hillside villas of the Renaissance cardinals and money lenders of Tuscany were too grand and showy for all but the most irrepressible of Hollywood's movie moghuls. When wandering about the parterres and cascades today of any sixteenth-century Italian gardens, one must surely be impressed by such grandeur and effect, while at the same time trying to imagine their everyday usage or calculating the number of gardeners needed to maintain such precise and elaborate layouts. Concerns like these must surely have given pause to even the wealthiest of California's touring tycoons of the early twentieth century. And the architects and landscape architects brought along to gather ideas and inspiration would have had the responsibility of creating an image of long ago, in faraway Tuscany or Lombardy, to be juxtaposed with the decade of the shimmy, blackbottom, speakeasies, and jazz. In this way, formal parterres were made to double as dance pavilions, terraces as putting greens, graveled carriageways as parking lots, and axially aligned reflecting ponds as swimming pools.

Some California architects achieved noteworthy success in this blending of time and place. Myron Hunt's Pasadena houses are still praiseworthy, as are the houses of Gordon Kaufmann and Wallace Neff, whose southern California mansions have become historic landmarks of Spanish Colonial Revival. Reginald Johnson and George Washington Smith both enjoyed the same level of popularity in Santa Barbara and Montecito. Perhaps more original in molding the Mediterranean idiom into a contemporary form were Irving Gill, whose remaining work can be seen in San Diego and La Jolla, and Frank Lloyd Wright, who built several houses in Los Angeles that reflect Moorish and Hispanic qualities.

Landscape architects likewise met the challenge of the twenties, producing elaborate Spanish and Italian gardens which are still regarded as outstanding examples of the art in California. Indeed, in the heady world of garden making, there was nothing quite like the Mediterranean California garden of the 1920s.

Below: Architect George Washington Smith's Montecito home and garden, 1928.

Opposite page: Casa del Herrero, Montecito, 1925-28. Principal axis from house to lower garden and paving detail. Ralph Stevens, landscape architect.

During a single decade, the garden was elevated in importance to that of the house, and huge sums were allocated—equaling or even exceeding the cost of the mansion—in creating the wondrous settings that reflected the opulence of the Old World. Set in the hills and above the coastline, these estates featured long vistas, walled and ballistraded parterres with bubbling fountains, molded concrete cascades to rival the stone-cut statuary of old, with shell-shaped basins, river gods, fetching water nymphs, colored beach pebbles of intricate design set in concrete floors, or glazed tile basins and runnels carrying water to pools below. Houses were usually sited to maximize views, often in L or U shape for the purpose of enclosing interior patios, which became the centers for both entertainment and family gathering. Typically these grand houses would include a series of outdoor rooms that the landscape architect created a variety of settings for differing activities. Summerhouses—glorietas, gazebos, temples—rose arbors, and secret gardens joined the more practical places made for swimming, tennis and court games, putting greens, and children's play areas. Most of all, however, the 1920s estate gardens were an attempt to create an image of romantic beauty in a faraway setting. Perhaps the moving picture industry was partly responsible for emphasizing this image, but it was also found in the literature and popular music of the times:

> *"Beside the garden wall,*
>
> *when stars are bright,*
>
> *You are in my arms,*
>
> *The nightingale tells his*
>
> *fairy tale,*
>
> *A paradise where roses*
>
> *bloom."* [26]

The leading landscape architects of this Mediterranean revival era include Charles Gibbs Adams, Paul Thiene, and A.E. "Archie" Hanson, all from southern California. They produced hard-edged, geometric gardens of a distinctly Italian Renaissance character, and were all particularly skilled at hillside design and engineering, using the irregularities of the natural topography to maximum effect.

Left: Wall detail.

Opposite: A modern touch provided to the gardens of the Alcázar, Córdoba.

Paul Thiene: Creating the Old World in the New

Born in Germany in 1880 and educated there, Paul Thiene came to California about 1910, finding work as a garden designer in San Diego's Panama-California Exposition where he eventually became head gardener. With the close of the fair, he headed for Los Angeles and later to Pasadena, where he began to practice landscape architecture, seeking clients who wished to build Spanish or Italian gardens. His early training as a garden designer in Germany, his experience in San Diego, and his grasp of California's ever broadening plant material palette helped establish his reputation. Working with Kate Sessions, San Diego's leading importer of ornamental plants, was no doubt of great benefit to Thiene. In his personal correspondence, he always mentioned his work at the exposition and the gardens he designed for the Doheny mansion in Beverly Hills, called Greystone, as his most important achievements.

Above: Paul G. Thiene, shortly after arriving in southern California, about 1910.

Opposite: The garden facade of the Getz estate in Beverly Hills reflects the Italian Renaissance with its cascading water feature and reflecting pool. Fan palms, however, are strictly southern Californian. The entry court is made of pre-cast concrete pavers with grass joints. Paul Thiene, landscape architect, 1923.

At Greystone, Thiene was faced not only with complex topographic changes, but also with a massive 46,000 square-foot house of French provincial design. Multileveled parterres, including a swimming pool, tennis courts, motor court, and various courtyards suggest a garden of many rooms, each with its own purpose and character. To accomplish all of this, considerable grading was required, excavation and filling of over 30,000 cubic yards of soil to get the site into a workable condition—all done by use of wheel barrow and hand shoveling, with some occasional dynamiting. Specimen trees were planted by the hundreds at Greystone, including deodar, Atlantic cedar, crape myrtle, olive, pepper, redwood, poplar, various pine species, California sycamore, and live oak. Thiene's own description of the garden reveals the overriding search for illusion so prevalent in those times:

"As we go down a twisting, shaded flagstone path, along banks planted with plumbago and chorizema, California holly or a clump of hydrangea...may brighten many positions of prominence. Enticed by the rippling of waters we suddenly find ourselves standing at the brink of a wonderful lake...gazing upward we perceive the supply in the form of a cascade...many, many feet above. Centuries might easily have elapsed, although in reality it is less than two years since the stream of crystal clear water started rushing down over its moss grown course." [27]

The house and grounds, although somewhat altered today, are now the property of the City of Beverly Hills, and the gardens may be visited daily.

Opposite: Lola Stake Thiene, Paul, Carleton, Paul Jr., on the Lodge Terrace of their Pasadena home, 1928.

Left: "La Collina," 1920 Beverly Hills estate, with gardens by Paul Thiene. Note use of water-conserving edging plants in foreground, poolside.

Above: Arrival courtyard of the Doheny mansion, called "Greystone" because of its imported gray granite and slate walls and roof. The gardens, by Paul Thiene, are open to the public. Built in 1925, this Beverly Hills mansion and its elaborate garden complex have served as background for countless Hollywood films, and for weddings and other 'photo opportunities.'

Eisner estate, west Los Angeles, 1925. Paul Thiene's use of Mediterranean form is evident in the pools and pre-cast concrete pavers, walls, and potted plants leading toward the entry. Garden facade (bottom) based on Islamic and Mediterranean themes generally.

Charles Gibbs Adams:

Remaking

the Patio

Another of the pioneer landscape architects to become established in the early years of the Mediterranean revival was Charles Gibbs Adams. Born in Los Angeles in 1884, he studied landscape architecture at the University of California, Berkeley, and then did a postgraduate tour of European gardens— even before it became de rigueur for wealthy industrialists. After opening an office in 1917 in Pasadena, he quickly established a reputation for carefully detailed residential design that effectively blended house and garden. Adams was perhaps the first of his generation to acknowledge fully the function and importance of the patio as the crux of the garden, as in the daily life of families during the pastoral age, and to translate that concept into contemporary

usage and form. He was also one of the first of his era to make substantial use of California's own native plants, often replacing earlier plantations of tropicals, eastern shrubs, and thirsty lawns. Bucking the tide of popular taste—since the nursery trade so overwhelmingly favored the frothy *exotics* from Australia, South America, and Africa—Adams believed thoroughly in the idea of using appropriate plants for southern California's climate and soils, and he defended his position extensively wherever there was an opportunity to be heard. A charming, witty speaker, Adams was regularly in demand as a lecturer on garden design, plant material, and local California history. Although a hobnob of film and stage folk, he lived modestly in South Pasadena, practicing his profession from the old adobe built in 1841 by Manuel Garfías near the location of Portolá's Charter Oak, on the Arroyo Seco in Pasadena.

Charles Gibbs Adams, possibly envisioning his future career, astride a California live oak in Marin County, on his twentieth birthday, 1904, and on Twin Peaks, San Francisco, 1912.

View of Silver Lake, Los Angeles, across a 1924 garden by Charles Gibbs Adams.

Adams's more notable gardens include many of the homes of the silent screen stars, as well as Cecil B. DeMille and publisher William Randolph Hearst, whose "castle" near San Simeon is to-day a popular tourist attraction. Although he wrote enthusiastically about the small patio garden, he is better known for his large estates in Los Angeles and the Santa Barbara area. The Henry Dater estate, occupying seventeen acres of wooded hillside in Montecito, is one of his best. Originally named *Dias Felices* when built in 1919 by Bertram Goodhue, the house overlooks a shaded valley from the brow of a low hill, down from which a series of stairs and parterres descend to a formal reflecting pool (actually the garden's reservoir) on axis from the upper garden. Renamed *Val Verde* by a later owner, the grounds were improved in the following decade by landscape architect Lockwood de Forest.

Above: Balustrade and fountain at "Arcady," the Montecito home of George Knapp, 1920s. Charles Gibbs Adams, landscape architect.

Top: The W.K. Kellogg mansion, with gardens designed by Charles Gibbs Adams, and later by Florence Yoch and Lucile Council. The cereal czar raised Arabian horses here during the 1920s and early 1930s. The 840 acre estate, including the mansion and grounds, is now the campus of California State Polytechnic University, Pomona.

A.E. Hanson:

Privacy

and Drama

A.E. "Archie" Hanson came to land-scape architecture by a more roundabout route. Born in Chino in 1894, the son of a nurseryman, he was somewhat the oppo-site of the urbane, well-traveled Adams. Trained in the trenches of agricultural field work, Hanson acquired his knowl-edge and appreciation for plants through hauling and digging them. In time, he found more lofty employment with Theodore Payne, the well-known horti-culturist, and Hanson gained a respect for Mediterranean and California native plant material while working in Payne's nurs-ery. Although lacking a formal education and untraveled, save for visits to the two California expositions of 1915, World War I provided him with an opportunity to

visit European gardens following hostilities there. Taking advantage of Payne's recommendations, Hanson visited Versailles and other classical French Formal gardens. Years later, dur-ing a break in the construction of the Harold Lloyd garden in Beverly Hills, he returned to Europe for a more profes-sional viewing of the gardens of Spain and Italy:

"We went to the Generalife. Every landscape architect should go there. It defies the imagination. The gardens of the Alhambra at Granada, and of that Moorish, Andalusian part of Spain— these are the kind of gardens we should have in southern California." [28]

Hanson was a natural designer, who usually arrived at a solution to clients' needs after a single site visit. For the many small gardens he designed between 1915 and 1920, he developed a basic approach:

"We would heavily screen the back and side property lines," he wrote, "so that the owners would have complete privacy. But then to add interest there would be some kind of little garden tucked away on the side...this added interest to the whole area." [29]

With the Great Depression cutting into his gilt-edged practice, Hanson went into community planning, but he is best remembered for his private gardens and particularly for those grand, romantic es-tates. Like Thiene and Adams he found an eager clientele among the entrepre-neurs of the moving picture world, com-pleting projects of great size and intricate detail. The most impressive of these— perhaps the largest and most elaborate garden attempted in those heady times— was made for Harold Lloyd on his 16 acre Benedict Canyon estate. The site itself was magnificent, with views to all sides and a long drainage valley at its base, running the length of the property line.

*Opposite Left: (from the book, **The California Gardens of A.E. Hanson**) 1927.*

1990 photos of restored gardens of Kirk Johnson estate in Montecito. The Wisteria covered arbor (below) and Italian balustrade (above), and stairway to lower garden (above left). A.E. Hanson, landscape architect.

GARDEN FOR MR & MRS. E. L. DOHENY

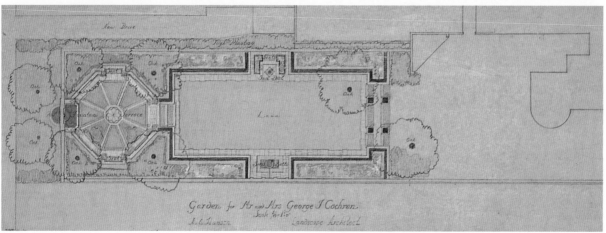

Garden for Mr and Mrs George J Cochran
A.E. Hanson   Landscape Architect

The mansion, by architect Sumner Spaulding, occupied the crest of the hill, and the long, meandering valley became a golf course along an artificial stream. The impressive entry drive bridged the valley and stream, then followed the rolling contours of the site, climbing eventually to a formal motor court. Between valley and hilltop, a series of Italianate parterres and cascades were constructed, conforming more to the natural topography than to any rigid, symmetrical plan. It was in this respect—following the natural contouring of the land rather than bowing to the dictates of Renaissance geometrics—that Hanson broke with his much admired Villa d'Este.

The Lloyd estate may well be the pinnacle of Hollywood's efforts to achieve in reality what had been so successfully constructed on film: *image into being*. It was, however, to be the last of its kind. The advent of talking pictures, in addition to the depression, made it increasingly difficult for Lloyd to maintain the elaborate gardens, although long after his film career had ended and nearly to the time of his death in 1971, he continued to show off the property to

1928 and 1929 sketches and plans by A.E. Hanson: Wallace Neff garden (opposite) in San Marino, Doheny garden in Beverly Hills (top), and the George Cochran garden in Los Angeles (above).

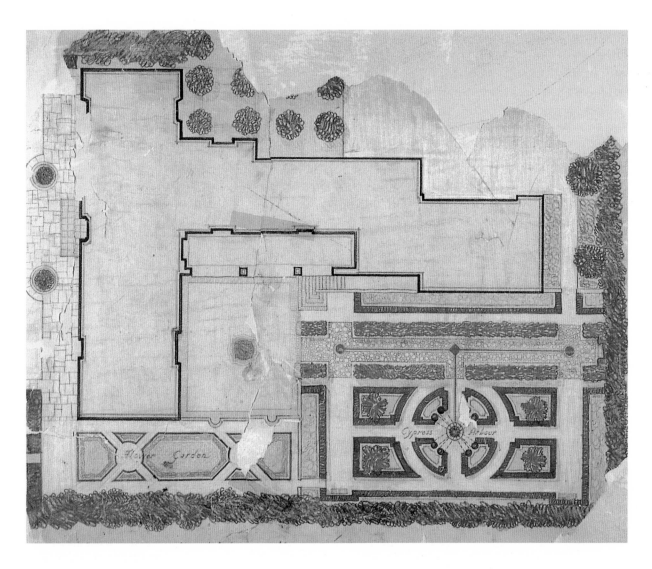

Flower Garden

Cypress Arbour

members of the press, traveling dignitaries, and Hollywood nabobs. At a tribute to Lloyd, before the estate was divided into acre lots and sold off, Roddy McDowell stated that Lloyd believed the garden to be his greatest accomplishment.

Hanson outlived many of his own large gardens as the depression and later housing development in southern California took their toll on California's large estates. In a letter from January, 1979, he wrote:

"I didn't think there were any (gardens) to show, except the Kirk B. Johnson garden (in Montecito). It has occurred to me that a garden I did in 1928 for an oil tycoon by the name of Lockhart might be of interest. Two years ago when I saw it, it was greatly run down and it was heartbreaking to see. The Getty Oil Company had owned the property for a number of years. Recently they gave it and a sum of money for its restoration to the City of Los Angeles. The house and grounds have been completely restored, and while I have not seen the finished work, I believe the grounds are almost in their original condition." [30] (This hoped-for restoration of the Lockhart garden was unfortunately less than successful, due in part to the wishes of the incumbant mayor.)

111

While lacking many of the technical skills required in his profession, Hanson thought of himself as the composer and leader of the orchestra, maintaining close contact with all of his projects, from drawing board to installation. Although most of his clients were wealthy owners of large estates, he personally admired the small, intimate enclosed gardens of Andalusian cities and saw their relevance to California:

"As you walked down the narrow streets and looked in through the front grille gate you saw a patio, or a little court. Every court had a small, shallow pool with a nozzle and a splash of water. Any of these pools could be put to good use in California." [31]

A number of other landscape architects were making names for themselves during this Mediterranean Revival era, including Ralph Stevens, Lockwood and Elizabeth de Forest in Santa Barbara, George Hall, Wilbur Cook, Jr., Ray Page, Frederick Law Olmsted, Jr., Ruth Shellhorn, Florence Yoch and Lucile Council, Ralph Cornell, Edward Huntsman-Trout, Harriet Wimmer, Katherine Bashford in the south, and Geraldine Knight Scott, Leland Vaughan, Bruce Porter in the north.

Opposite: Terrace of the Kirk Johnson estate, Montecito.

Below: Rendering of the Kirk Johnson estate in Montecito, built in 1928-29 by architect George Washington Smith. Landscape architect, A.E. Hanson.

Florence Yoch:
Theatrics
and
Capricci

Florence Yoch was fortunate to have had parents who believed in education for women and could afford to provide it for their daughter. She therefore received the best training available, at three universities, in landscape architecture and the classics, followed by an extensive travel program in Europe for the purpose of studying the outstanding historic gardens. When she considered herself to be sufficiently grounded in the basics of Mediterranean design and plantings, she

returned to California and opened a practice of landscape architecture in Pasadena, in 1918, taking on clients through family connections at first and later by way of a growing reputation for design precision, originality, plant knowledge, and skillful execution of plans. In an age when landscape architects made their mark largely through painstaking attention to detail and scrupulous on-site supervision, Yoch probably outdid them all. Intelligent and well-read, she would not let herself become trapped into rote-like copying of the Italian gardens she so admired. Instead, she strayed further from the original than any of her contemporaries, breaking across established sight-lines for effect and thwarting symmetry whenever a more lyrical composition might be at hand.

No doubt influenced by author Edith Wharton's glowing praise of Italian Renaissance gardens, Yoch eschewed their grand formality, which had so conquered her fellow travelers, concentrating more on enhancing the effects of simple spaces that were comfortably scaled to human use—often with a dash of her own brand of theatrics. Indeed, it is entirely possible that she perceived a heightened, romantic aura in the aged, ruined state of the old gardens, qualities perhaps missing from them in their own time—and qualities with which she sought to infuse her own gardens. It is apparent in Wharton's writing, as well as Yoch's designs—a sense of *capricci.*

"The garden lover," wrote Wharton, "should not content himself with a vague enjoyment of old Italian gardens but should try to extract from them principles which may be applied at home. He should observe, for instance, that the Italian garden was meant to be lived in— a use which at least in America the modern garden is seldom put." [32]

Florence Yoch was born in Illinois in 1890, and moved to Santa Ana with her family while still very young. She is described by those who knew her best—family members and clients alike—as being strong willed, certain of herself in matters of design, and unchangeable. As a sensitive scrutinizer of the most minuscule detail, she was actually quite capable of changing her mind and did so often while on project sites, as one might move furniture around, until satisfied with the foliage textures, the right amount of light, and the shape and character of enclosed spaces. Plan view drawing, Humphrey Repton once explained, was a poor means of developing a garden design. Although a capable draftsman herself, Yoch would probably have agreed.

Opposite: Florence Yoch in 1964. Below: The topiary garden at "Il Brolino." Above: Detail of "Il Brolino," the Stewart garden in Montecito, by Yoch and Council.

In 1925, Yoch took on Lucile Council as a partner, an arrangement that lasted for the remainder of their lives. Together they incorporated the skill and technique of design, a keen awareness of plant usage and a growing business acumen necessary to carry on their practice. Although the partnership was devoted nearly exclusively to private garden design, Yoch's sense of place, her special talent for augmenting a garden composition, led to commissions to design movie sets, the best remembered being *Gone With The Wind*. A biography of her life by James Yoch was published in 1989.

Above: Reflection pool in a 1920s estate in San Marino, by Yoch and Council. The "Oak Room" at the same San Marino estate (below).

Opposite: Patio of the Athenaeum, Caltech, Pasadena, by Florence Yoch and Lucile Council.

Edward Huntsman-Trout: Innovation and Practicality

From all accounts, the twenties were exciting years for California. Great fortunes were amassed, resulting in great expenditures for all the good things in life, including gardens. But California had also become a pleasant and rewarding place for those of more modest means as well, and several landscape architects of the period concerned themselves more with the welfare of the middle class homeowner, with his Spanish bungalow and 60-foot by 100-foot lot. One such designer was Edward Huntsman-Trout.

Born in Canada in 1889, Trout began his practice in California during the early 1920s concentrating on residential garden design. Soft spoken and articulate, yet strong willed and resolute in his design concepts, he understood precisely where his abilities lay and rarely veered from his life-long love for designing small gardens. Like Adams, he attended the University of California—before the landscape architecture program was initiated there—and studied horticulture and architecture. In 1913, he went to Harvard, becoming the first Californian to receive professional training in landscape architecture. While there he was introduced to the Beaux-Arts principles of design, the heavy-handed nineteenth century European formalism still being taught at that time in American schools of architecture.

Like others before him, Trout embraced sharp-edged geometric landscape form, but in his hands it resulted in a more practical, more logical method than the rules of rhythm, symmetry, and style would have foreseen. Perhaps from his earlier architectural training, as well as from living in California, designing the garden as an enclosed extension of the house seemed natural and obvious to him. In respecting the place of the patio, Trout was more resolute than most of those who had preceded him. The small garden became his milieu, the patio a walled, private room, often with a hard floor. He resisted using grass, except at a distance from the house and patio, and he disliked front yards altogether, unless some practical purpose for them could be found. He was probably the era's most determined designer of useful outdoor rooms, writing:

"With all the courts and patios which our current predilection for the Mediterranean sort of expression is giving us, so few of them succeed with just the right balance of shelter and airiness, of sunlight and shade, of enclosure and space. When these wants are all satisfied in one, the garden is truly what it should be—another room in the home." [33]

In his efforts to design gardens that were consistently useful and private, as well as attractive, Trout lived by three self-determined rules: First, satisfy the clients' needs—not in mindless obedience to requirements, but in getting to know them and understanding their way of life. In this way, he became a friend to the people he worked for, spending time with his clients throughout the garden's development and afterwards, in order to judge its success. Second, understand the site. Trout made careful studies of the drainage, topography, views, and sun angles, always aware of temperature variations and wind conditions so as to maximize the year round usefulness of the outdoor spaces. Third, simplify. In an address to the landscape architecture students at the University of California, Berkeley, in 1963, he said:

"It has always been my firm conviction that the planning we do should seek the obvious, the straight forward answer, the least common denominator, the inevitable. I like it best when what I have done seems not to have been contrived. It was just there." [34]

Above: View into the patio of a Los Angeles garden designed by Edward Huntsman-Trout. Opposite: Edward Huntsman-Trout, 1957.

Trout rarely became involved in the great estates of the twenties, but when designing large projects like the campus of Scripps College (with architect Gordon Kaufmann), he attempted to achieve the same goals of human scale, straightforward and useful enclosed space, and overall integration between gardens and architecture. "The characteristic elements of our out-of-door creation," he wrote, "are the soil it springs from, the sky that domes it over, the greenery that flourishes there. Grass for a carpet, shrubs and hedges for walls, trees for shade, flowers to decorate the whole." [35]

Before the stock market crash of 1929, other eclectic architectural styles had begun to appear in southern California, including Dutch Colonial, English Tudor, and French Provincial. In dealing with these, Trout showed his flexibility in design and choice of materials, but more importantly he never allowed eclectics or mere style to alter his three rules of design method.

He was a slight, pleasant man with a quiet, mild manner. He did not search out clients but took them as they came to him, one at a time. He understood his strengths, working steadily at residential garden design until his death at age 85, in 1974.

"I keep my nose, professionally, mostly in the backyards." [36]

Opposite: Same garden as previous page, seen from street entry.

Below: Drafting Details for the Jay Paley estate in Holmby Hills, by Huntsman-Trout.

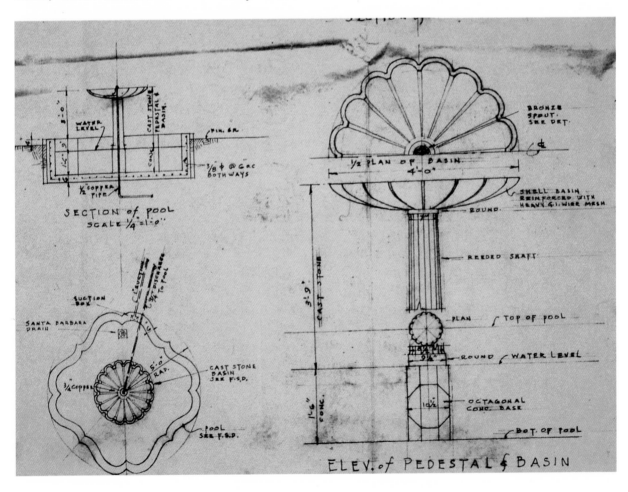

The de Forests: Breaking the Mold

To the north, Lockwood de Forest and his wife Elizabeth were developing a successful practice of garden design in and around Santa Barbara during the 1920s. Their work is distinguished by its precise, careful detail, particularly in plant design and the use of stonework, but most of all for its subtle, as well as practical departure from traditional Mediterranean symmetry. Lockwood de Forest, a curly-headed, amiable fellow, who liked fast, open cars and good company, made close friends of his clients, and bent the rules of traditional geometry in order to better serve their immediate needs. His re-design of the gardens at Val Verde (by then the home of his long-time friend and art connoisseur, Wright Ludington) in 1926 demonstrates a keen sensitivity to both the original Adams' design and the realistic needs of the new owners.

The son of a successful New York artist-inventor, de Forest was born in New York City in 1896, coming in his youth to California, where his family had frequently spent the winters. He first became interested in landscape architecture while serving in the Army in World War I, after which he enrolled for

a time in the evolving landscape architecture program at Berkeley. Leaving the university dissatisfied and without a degree, he nonetheless, sought out a former teacher Ralph Stevens who was practicing landscape architecture at the time in Montecito and Santa Barbara. Known to his associates as "Grumpy," Stevens proved to be a difficult instructor for the rather carefree and impatient de Forest, and within a few months the younger man departed for Europe to study the gardens of Italy and Spain. His practice of landscape architecture in Santa Barbara began in earnest in 1920, and following his marriage in 1925 to Elizabeth Kellam, the de Forest partnership continued until his death in 1947. Elizabeth practiced on her own for another thirty years, concentrating on small gardens and acting as mentor to local aspiring landscape architects. Both Elizabeth and Lockwood de Forest are memorialized in inscriptions outside the Santa Barbara Museum of Art, whose gardens they designed.

Like Yoch and Trout, the de Forests were innovators and experimenters in geometric form, and as such were amongst the first in California to point the way towards a more original garden form. In their hands, the Italian Renaissance had already become difficult to recognize—and a new California garden no longer dependent on symmetry and measured geometry seemed imminent.

Above: Reflecting pool and reservoir for "Val Verde," Montecito. Gardens by Charles Gibbs Adams, later additions by Lockwood de Forest.

Opposite page: Elizabeth and Lockwood de Forest in "The Buffalo," their working auto, here on an outing in the hills north of Santa Barbara, about 1934. Rear passenger is probably Richard Brimer (top). The swimming pool at "Val Verde," added by de Forest, is enclosed in turn by an avenue of lilies, a Greek key hedge, and a double row of plastered columns (bottom).

Raymond Page: Recognizing the Profession

Another important figure to evolve from the Mediterranean Revival tradition was Raymond Page (pictured above in 1987). Born in Nebraska in 1895, he came west with his parents as a child, and although he received little training in landscape architecture, his early studies in art helped prepare him for a career that, in his recollection, seemed to be there in California just waiting for him.

Beverly Hills was being developed in 1919 by the Rodeo Land and Water Company, with help from the Beverly Hills Nursery, who gave Page his first job. Soon he found himself busy designing gardens for the newly rich and famous of cinema—Clark Gable (with whom he often went hunting), Jack Benny (no skinflint in private life, given to sudden whims in the garden), Gloria Swanson, Douglas Fairbanks, Charlie Chaplin (for whom he designed a garden as a surprise gift from Theda Bara), George Burns and Gracie Allen, and Donna Reed.

Page's greatest accomplishment, in his own opinion, was the establishing of licensing for the profession of landscape architecture. The need occurred to him while serving as a professional witness during a civil action suit that involved the improper grading of a road. When the defense attorney was able to ridicule

Page's professional testimony—relying on a dictionary definition of *landscape architect*—he realized something must be done to acquire status for the many men and women in practice, and for their clients as well. Through his untiring efforts, California became the first state in 1954 to establish a licensure requirement for landscape architects.

Page was also responsible, along with Mrs. Valley Knudsen, for organizing The Los Angeles Beautiful movement during the early 1950s. Much of the landscape development of Beverly Hills, including its street tree program and its city parks, is also the work of Raymond Page.

Opposite: Ray Page in 1987

Below: Ray Page designed this enclosed garden in Beverly Hills for actress Donna Reed, pictured here with her husband.

Courtyard Gardens

A new kind of patio garden emerged in the Los Angeles area during the twenties which was completely in keeping with both the stylistic fashion of the times and the desire for enclosed privacy in outdoor living. This was the courtyard complex, a somewhat fanciful architectural aggregation of apartment units, loosely joined so as to achieve maximum opportunity for patio gardens in the niches and spaces between

stuccoed walls. Outlandishly theatrical, featuring every known Moorish architectural device, they quite naturally appealed to cinema people, their friends, and hangers-on. They were also very successfully designed, offering a wide variety of living units to tenants and creating useful gathering places and private patios. Carefully separated from the adjacent streets and sidewalks by walls and hedges, these complexes made efficient use of outdoor spaces no matter how small. They became miniaturized oases, like the Spanish patios that A. E. Hanson so admired in the narrow streets of Córdova.

Forerunner to the condominium movement of the 1960s, the courtyard complex was neither single family, nor duplex, nor anything like the long, dull rows of apartment blocks that had saturated so many residential neighborhoods throughout most American cities during the late nineteenth century. Courtyard housing, especially in Pasadena, Hollywood, and West Los Angeles during the twenties, was anything but dull, with names like The Garden of Allah and El Patio Del Moro to prove it.

Opposite: Central fountain with cherub, Town Club courtyard in Pasadena, by Yoch and Council.

Left: The courtyard apartments of the 1920s, forerunners of today's condominiums. Arthur Zwebell built many of them, mostly in the Spanish or Moorish idiom, and all of them were provided with charming, enclosed patios.

Walter and Pierpont Davis were early pioneers of the courtyard complex, with projects of Mediterranean design dating from about 1915. But the principal interpreter of the concept was a builder named Arthur Zwebell, who scattered courtyard projects throughout Hollywood and West Los Angeles during the decade, with names like Villa Primavera (West Hollywood, 1923), Andalusia (West Hollywood, 1926), Casa Laguna (Los Feliz, 1928), and El Cabrillo (Hollywood, 1928). Many have been lost to high-rise development in recent years, but others—like the Andalusia, with its patio garden, tiled entries and fountain—have been lovingly restored.

During the depression and perhaps in some ways because of it, innovative housing in California was not an uncommon phenomenon. Following the success of courtyard complexes came the most comprehensive housing development project of the entire era—Palos Verdes Estates (now Rancho Palos Verdes)—which commenced construction in the late twenties and continued being built throughout most of the depression. Planned by the Olmsted Brothers in Boston, principally Frederick Law Olmsted, Jr., who moved here to see the project through to completion, Palos Verdes included not only intelligently sited housing, but also a series of carefully planned neighborhood commercial centers, parks, and schools. Its street system was engineered to preserve the natural integrity of the hilly terrain. There was also a carefully drawn covenant intended to assure that the Mediterranean character of the community would be permanently retained. With some modification, the original codes still prevail and Palos Verdes remains a highly desired community where walking and human-scale planning take precedence over the maximizing of auto traffic and parking—solutions that have debased so many towns in recent years.

Above: View into courtyard garden of "Andalusia," by Arthur Zwebell, Los Angeles.

Arthur Zwebell's Los Angeles area courtyard gardens: opposite—Rosewood, top—El Cabrillo.

Olmsted also designed the grounds of many of the new Mediterranean houses that were built during the 1920s at Palos Verdes Estates, including Villa Narcissa, the home of the peninsula's original owner and principal developer, Frank A. Vanderlip. Still under family ownership, the villa's remaining thirteen acres continue to express their Tuscan inspired origins, particularly in respect to the careful choice of water conserving plant materials reminiscent of a handsome Florentine villa of the sixteenth century.

Baldwin Hills Village (now The Village Green, pictured pg. 238) was another experiment in housing and attached private gardens constructed during the depression, and has also proven to be successful. Its plan, by Robert Alexander and Reginald Johnson, attempts to maximize outdoor open space, as well as to provide individual gardens, while nearly doubling the overall density on the 64-acre site. To achieve this goal, the architects reduced the number of streets and eliminated the waste space of conventional front yards, combining the street entry areas with vehicular storage and service needs.

"To tame the car," said Alexander, "we took our inspiration from the superblock concept derived from turn-of-the-century British planners like Ebenezer Howard. The basic idea was to keep the 64 acre estate intact, not sliced up by streets." [37]

Opposite: Courtyard at end of entry drive, "Val Verde."

Above: The Italian influence is apparent in the terminal fountain of the Bowling Green, the Huntington garden, San Marino.

Today we can look back on the Mediterranean Revival garden and the landscape architects who created them, with both nostalgia and forbearance. True, they are largely derivative of other places and times, and because of the influences of film-star clients, further augmented by illusion, drama, and romantic imagery. They are also an honest attempt to re-define the past, in search of the heritage left them from that early legacy of the simple, enclosed, functional patio.

IV.

The Modern Garden

Observe always that everything
is the result of change,
and get used to thinking that
there is nothing nature loves so well
as to change her existing forms,
and to make new ones like them.

Marcus Aurelius (121-180 A.D.)

Southern California Mediterranean style residence.
Designed by Peridian, Rae Price landscape architect.

Aside from the good fortune of the film industry's dream merchants, California suffered disproportionately during the early years of the Depression, or so it seemed to those who had sacrificed and gambled in coming west with expectations fostered by the railroad and real estate promoters and all the others who had made promises of a golden place of eternal springtime—of orange blossoms perfuming the air, snow capped mountain peaks set against an azure sky, and endless stretches of sparkling beaches. California's 1930 population of over five million had a considerable dependence on midwestern and east coast markets for the products of her young industries. On arriving in southern California for the first time, W.C. Fields is supposed to have said: "The whole place stank of oranges." It would not be the worst thing to be said of southern California during the next couple of decades.

But the fates that deal in calamities were not yet finished with the Golden State. In 1933, there came a devastating earthquake to the resort-turned-oil-boom-town of Long Beach, followed shortly after by the unprecedented and wholly unwelcomed in-migration tide of destitute families from the drought ravaged farmlands of northern Texas, Kansas, and Oklahoma. California, the real estate promoters' paradise, was becoming the refuge of the destitute.

Residence in Malibu, landscape architect, Gerald Pearson (Peridian).

"California's a garden of Eden,"

sang Woody Guthrie,

"A paradise to live in or see,

But believe it or not,

You won't find it so hot

If you ain't got that do re mi." [38]

Nevertheless, it was the ideal environment for the coming of the modern California garden. The garden era that we enjoy in the Golden State today owes much to the stagnant economy of the depression years—in ways that resemble the evolution of the Bauhaus in a flattened Germany during the years following World War I. Landscape architects, particularly those who had been making a comfortable living planning large, Mediterranean gardens for the rich and powerful, had to streamline services, reduce paperwork and correspondence, broaden the base of clientele to include more modest projects, and learn to utilize inexpensive, mass produced building materials. Most important, they had to learn to simplify, to design efficiently and on a smaller scale—that is, learn to seek out the middle class client on his small suburban lot. In short, they had to learn to do more with less—or look for another way to earn a living.

Some landscape architects closed their offices and sought employment elsewhere; for instance, in various park programs sponsored by the state and federal governments, in city park and planning departments, or in comparable public work. Some, like A.E. Hanson, went into development planning and others simply found other lines of work, or like Paul Thiene, retired early.

Opposite top: Detail of a garden in Woodside by Thomas Church, 1939.

Opposite bottom: A Hillsborough garden designed by Church.

Thomas Church: Reinventing The Garden

A few landscape architects continued to design private gardens, however, and fortunately for California, one of these was Thomas Dolliver Church. Along with other stalwarts unwilling to abandon the garden, he was determined to carry on the kind of landscape architectural practice that he most preferred. To succeed in this, he would be obliged to re-examine all that he had learned in school, as well as to reconsider the garden in a broader, more encompassing prospect. Eventually, this lead him to a re-interpretation of the very concept of garden, infusing it with many of the ordinary routines of household life, as well as the more aesthetic functions and qualities that only a garden is expected to possess. And in doing so he

discovered, by experimentation, a wholly new medium of expression, practical, as well as beautiful, that could be made to fit any client's budget or shrunken estate.

Space came first in Church's process of design. The outdoor living room—that enclosed and formalized patio of the twenties—became the outdoor *everything* room. The garden was no longer to be seen as being *outdoors* somewhere, or even being a transition between indoors and out. It became a fully integrated essential in an expanded living space. Of this effort to integrate house and garden, Church wrote:

"Outdoor living in an enclosed courtyard, an old Spanish custom, provides the ultimate in privacy, protection and accessibility. The court is a center for family living. The main rooms of the house lead into it, and it is easily served from the kitchen. Wide sliding doors can be opened to a breeze or closed when it's windy." [39]

Church began his California practice by opening a small office in San Francisco in 1929. He had studied landscape architecture at the University of California, then attended Harvard for graduate work. Following his degree, like so many other pre-depression artists, architects, and landscape architects, he embarked on the "Grand Tour" of Europe's museums, palaces, and gardens, to learn first-hand—as was the tradition of his time— the bases upon which beaux arts training in the arts had been built. This method obliged design students to measure and copy the accepted architectural antecedents of the late nineteenth century, works on a rather grand and formal scale, rather than to explore new forms and methods. When he returned to the United States, he worked in the east for a short time, did a year of teaching at the University of Illinois, before settling down in San Francisco. At this fateful

juncture in his career, the stock market crash was only weeks away, with all of its grim images of unemployment, soup lines, and somber, unsmiling faces on every corner of downtown San Francisco—and for that matter, the world over. For Church it proved to be a most providential time to start a practice in garden design.

Opposite: Thomas Dolliver Church at age 40, with his ever-present pruning shears.

This page: One of Thomas Church's rare southern California gardens (about 1955). This home in Duarte illustrates his ability to connect interior and garden, and to develop the activity area that occurs in this transition area. The blending of turf and aggregate paving in broad, sweeping curves became a design motif with which he was long associated.

Misfortune begets opportunity, and so it was for young Thomas Church who saw the need to search out a new, broader clientele base—and a new approach to designing gardens. He realized that in order to make a living as a designer of gardens he would have to be able to offer these clients something more than mere beauty, luxury, and tasteful surroundings. On greatly reduced lot sizes, flexibility and practicality become more important, and in providing more useful gardens on a smaller scale, he realized that he would also have to address the individual and personal interests of the occupants. Church's determination to meet the requirements of these depression-era homeowners became the key to his success in these early, difficult years of practice. Indeed, it became the primary aspect of his approach to each residential project: What do these people want to do in the garden? The titles of his two books testify to this: *Gardens Are For People* and *Your Private World.*

Probably because of this self-avowed practicality in the design of gardens, his work seems to lack a consistency of style— a kind of signature, like that of certain architects and other designers, by which their work is readily identifiable. In this respect, Church was clearly swimming against the current of modern design, whose principal advocates often gave little notice to the wishes of their clients. Church was too homespun, too modest, too dedicated to his client to be caught up in the purists' abstract search for ideal form, which motivated the design process of most modern era architects.

"The owner, who is to use and pay for the garden, must be heard. Any tendency to design for design's sake, to create a pattern within which the owners must live according to rules set by the designer, is headed for frustration, if not disaster." [40]

However, a number of approaches which he developed tend to identify his work: the rhythmic, sawtooth border, the asymmetric geometry, the deliciously sweeping arcs of lawn and interrelated paving, planters and groundcover beds, the backless benches that form a force-line or fix the division between areas, the broad, angular decks that pull the living

Opposite: A Woodside garden, 1953. Owners instructed Church to design a swimming pool to provide easy observation of children in the water.

Above: Church at work in his office at 402 Jackson St., San Francisco, the year prior to his death in 1978. An old warehouse for spices during the 19th century, it provided his business needs for over 40 years— above an antique shop. Church's employees insisted that the aroma of far eastern spices continued to permeate the place, if ever so subtly, throughout his long tenure there.

room floor into the garden, with openings for trees to punch through, the
freestanding garden screens that eschew
corners. To some critics, these devices
would seem to denote formula-driven
solutions used to achieve quick and easy
results. For Church, however, the forms
of the garden never preceded the concept,
but grew out of it. Here, for example, in
his advice to would-be garden designers:

"Look carefully at your site before
you sigh and place the house square to
the property line with the living room
on the street and the kitchen and garage at the rear. Rooms can go any-
where you want them for the right
amount of sun at the right time of the
year. Wings of the house can protect
garden areas. If you want large areas of
glass, be wary of south and west

exposures...your pleasure will be di-
minished if you have to pull heavy
drapes at four o'clock." [41]

Therefore, in preparing garden plans,
his approach was invariably to determine
the owner's wishes and to take note of the
conditions of the site—its orientation, topography, drainage, views, existing trees,
and all other features.

But for all his pragmatic advice, Church
is best remembered today for his pioneer-
ing of the modern garden in California. It
is an original art form, having evolved
with the assistance of many sources,
including formalistic Spanish and Italian
gardens, early California mission and
rancho gardens, and the gardens that
derive from the International Movement
of Europe—particularly the Bauhaus and
the art deco style from 1930s Paris.

Church gave credit to all such sources, and was certainly influenced by them in his work. It is clear that he understood the basic principles of modernism—the freedoms of expression that is offered—but he sought his own path in achieving its goals, and he described his process of design in straight-forward language, filled with humor and pithy advice. This adaptive method is suggested in his approach to the design of the 1948 Kirkham garden in San Francisco:

"The original garden...was a square plot with a shed across the rear of the property. The garden now seems twice as big because the static lines of the

original rectangle have been changed, the moving lines of the curve play against the angular forms on the opposite side." [42]

The breaking of this "static rectangle", which had been the basic garden form of the 1920s, allowed Church to create illusions of greater size, to suggest movement and direction, and to impose a sense of curiosity—the wondering what lies ahead, just around the edge of the shrub border. This altered geometry illustrates his ability to visually enlarge outdoor space, give it movement and direction, and most of all, to perceive a solution based on clients' requirements and the characteristics of the site, rather than depending upon established formulas of form and style.

The Kirkham garden, San Francisco. A small city lot on an old rectangular garden plan, which in 1948 was reorganized by Church along a diagonal axis. As it looked shortly after completion in 1948 (above). By adding a new wood deck at the level of the living room, and removing half of the old tool shed in order to make a shaded retreat at the rear property line, Church was able to achieve an expanding sense of space, a new direction, and implied visual movement.

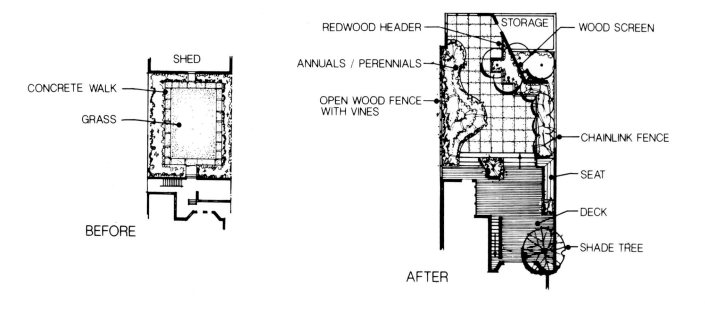

SHED

CONCRETE WALK

GRASS

BEFORE

REDWOOD HEADER

ANNUALS / PERENNIALS

OPEN WOOD FENCE
WITH VINES

STORAGE

WOOD SCREEN

CHAINLINK FENCE

SEAT

DECK

SHADE TREE

AFTER

Always the experimenter in form, Church designed the Martin's beach garden on the coast near Aptos, by making an enclosed space from two manufactured houses which had to be lifted over the cliff onto the beach below. The resulting garden was a symbolic conjunction of land and sea—and one of the most photographed gardens of California. The Martin beach garden and the Donnell garden, near Sonoma, (designed with Larry Halprin in 1948) are probably Church's best known and best loved modern gardens.

In Church's hands, a specimen tree became a pivotal point around which a spatial sequence could be organized; an existing wall that was seen as an intrusion might become a theatrical backdrop; a steep slope could become the opportunity for a broad, free-flowing deck extending from the living room with openings left for trees to poke through. Using hedges, vines, imaginative fence design, and varied surfaces, he choreographed the garden's circulation, visual progression, stopping places, and activity centers. Instead of hard, ninety-degree corners on fences and walls, Church often left them open-ended, or freestanding, giving the suggestion of extended property lines and connection with the larger landscape— the distant hills, the adjacent orange grove, or simply the next door neighbor's fine old live oak. Corners work well enough inside the house, but in the garden they become static stopping places, interruptions to visual flow and connection. A garden must continue to draw the eye from place to place, making one curious. "The eye prefers to move around a garden on lines that are provocative, never end in dead corners." [43]

Just as a living room seems larger when properly furnished, Church's gardens expand visually with the adroit use of free-standing screens, sharply delineated changes in level, sweeping curves, sawtoothed edges, extended planter walls, potted specimen plants, a variety of paving textures and colors, and carefully selected plantings for shade, contrast, color, depth, composition, and accent. With overhead structures and proper furnishings, a small backyard would be transformed into an expansive and beautiful outdoor entertainment center.

In breaking with Mediterranean traditions, Church was being neither abusive nor ignorant of the past. Certainly he was fully aware of the long precedent

therein for treating the garden both as an outdoor room and as an integral part of the house. In the introduction to *Gardens Are For People,* he wrote:

"The Egyptians planned their houses and gardens together...the Romans knew all about it, the Greeks had a word for it, and the Renaissance Italians developed it to a fine art...the garden was a transitional stage, saving them from stepping from their house to nature in the raw." [44]

In opposition to this concept of the garden as architecture, was the Romantic, Picturesque, or Naturalistic land-

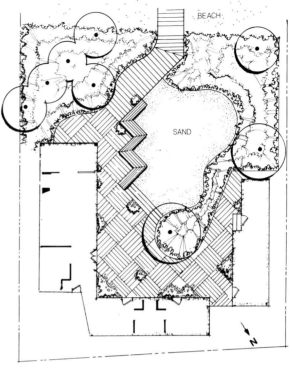

scape, variations of which reached their zenith in eighteenth-century England under the hand of Capability Brown and his followers. Church appreciated their contributions to garden design, crediting them with many of the ideas and devices for which he found a modern application. In describing the Robert Bush garden in Palo Alto, which abutted the rolling, natural terrain of a dairy ranch, he wrote:

Left and Above: The Martin beach garden at Aptos, perhaps Church's most photographed work.

145

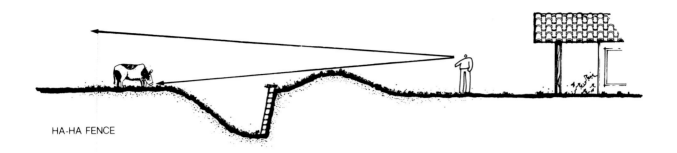

HA-HA FENCE

"In 18th-century England cattle grazed on public land and were a constant part of every landscape. To keep them out of the pleasure grounds and still see the flowing meadow and woods, a ditch with a fence at the bottom called a ha-ha was used...so the fence was lowered into a ditch at the property line...Someone else feeds the cows. The Bushes look at them." [45]

Before the stock market collapse, when Church began his San Francisco practice, the accepted garden style remained Mediterranean Revival and his earliest projects reflect this influence. The changes that began to affect garden design, and for that matter the entire world of art, cannot be laid entirely at the foot of the Great Depression. Modernism had earlier origins, as Church had

learned in his post-graduate junket to Europe in the 1920s. Certainly the architects he worked with, like William Wurster, proved influential. And although Church engaged very little in the stylistic and philosophic dialogue of the times, he was nonetheless aware of the broad changes occurring in the arts and in architecture. He was also a stubbornly individualistic designer—creative, original, and pragmatic in his approach to each project, and as such, was wary of style-generated change. He described the new mode as: "brave attempts to break the bond of eclecticism." He added, "modern can be revived as an honest word when we realize that modernism is not a goal but a broad highway." [46]

Opposite: Thomas Church in his San Francisco garden.

Left: In this Bay Area patio, Church demonstrates the transition between house and garden, privacy of enclosure, practicality—in a somewhat formal design.

Garrett Eckbo and Modern Form

Above: Garrett Eckbo at his home in Wonderland Park, Los Angeles, 1959.

The influences of modern art surrounded Church in the early 1930s and provided him with much of the inspiration, as well as the practical ideas needed for extrapolating the modern California garden. But he was not alone. In the south, Florence Yoch and Edward Huntsman-Trout had already begun the process of disengaging garden geometry from axiality and the bilateral symmetry of the Mediterranean garden, and in Santa Barbara, Lockwood and Elizabeth de Forest were also experimenting in ways to lessen the rigidity of axial composition. Others may also have contributed to creating an original California style, but it was to fall to Garrett Eckbo to fully develop the process and to set forth its principles and method.

Like Church, Eckbo studied landscape architecture at the University of California and later at Harvard. After leaving Berkeley in 1935, and following a brief stint as garden designer for Armstrong's Nursery in Ontario, he entered the graduate program at Harvard in the fall of 1936—a few months before the arrival there of Walter Gropius, founder of Germany's Bauhaus and leader of the modern movement in the arts and architecture. Gropius had come to Harvard seeking a more receptive environment for his design philosophy than Nazi Germany had provided him.

148

He intended to infuse Harvard and the art community in general with the ideas that had already begun to revolutionize the process of architectural design structure in Europe, with his collective design approach. It was a most propitious time for a young, open-minded California landscape architect to find himself in the Halls of Ivy.

Left and Right: This post-war modern house built in the hills of southern California, encloses the garden (by Garrett Eckbo) by emphasizing the indoor-outdoor transition of house and garden—in the California tradition.

Top: In this small Los Angeles garden, Eckbo introduces forty five degree angles and the clean, sparse structure of early post-modernism.

Above: This Palm Springs garden, by Francis Dean (Eckbo's partner), provides the owners with a full panorama of near and distant vistas—from the bedroom.

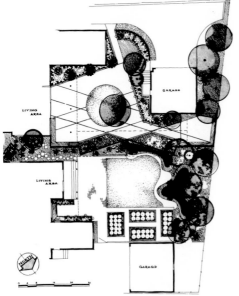

As chairman of the architecture department, Gropius set out at once to introduce the principles of organic process that had been the foundation of his Bauhaus collaboratives in Weimar and Dressau. Deploring the beaux-arts tradition that had for so long undergirded the faculty and the established architectural community of the east coast, he set out to reorder the entire creative process of American design. And as might have been expected, it was the students—at Harvard as well as Yale and other American schools—who were the first to embrace modernism.

As interpreted by Gropius and his close associate Marcel Breuer, modern design was a method of deriving structured form from the conditions of the site, its orientation, the available materials, the stated function of the program, and the absolute need for the form and character of the finished building to honestly reflect its purpose. Modern design also involved a collaborative effort; the selfless input from many minds, many disciplines, in a total composition that extended from the deeply conscientious and principled realization of the structural envelope to the smallest of its enclosed details—the teapot, the cups and saucers carefully arranged on the smooth, clean-edged white table which echoed its surroundings. Modernism embraced all that was functional and organic, and was therefore a rejection of historic precedents, predetermined order of Classic form, and for that matter, anything that had already been done and named.

Left: According to Eckbo, "these gardens were designed together to enhance the spatial form of each. The angled wall straddles the property line." (from a letter to the author).

Modernism, as explained by Gropius, meant starting afresh, literally from zero, and it was expected that space and form would evolve in a natural way as determined by a building's intended use. Thus, the eventual form would be a result of the process of resolving a building's various functions—quite unlike beaux arts form, which follows preconceived rules governing measure and proportion, regardless of a building's purpose.

The seeds of modernism that influenced Garrett Eckbo first appeared in Europe in the late nineteenth century's art nouveau movement—an initial reaction against the seemingly endless variations of Classicism. But the modernist ideal moved rapidly into the early twentieth century, taking shape in the many industrial projects following World War I, interpreting the social conscience of Europe in everything from dinnerware and street posters to mass housing programs and urban reform. Along with Gropius came other significant interpreters: LeCorbusier in France, Ludwig Mies van der Rohe in the Netherlands and Germany (and later Chicago), Richard Neutra in Germany and California.

Modernist painters who led the way toward rethinking the visual arts included Paul Klee, Wassily Kandinsky, Georges Braque, and Pablo Picasso. Piet Mondrian, along with others in the Netherlands, developed a totally non-objective method for interpreting form and color, which he called *de stijl* (the style). But the culmination of modern art in its most industrialized form was achieved in Paris, in 1925, at the *Exposition Internationale des Arts Decoratifs et Industriels Modernes*, which soon came to be known as art deco. A second and far more elaborate exposition was held there in 1937, from which the modern art and architecture movement in United States drew strength. Thus, modern architecture arrived somewhat timidly at first, and then with the simultaneous appearances of the second wave of art deco and Gropius at Harvard, it gained a sweeping following in the architectural academies across much of the land, as well as in New York City, Miami Beach, and Los Angeles. The uproar caused by this transplanted European movement, called the International Style when it reached American shores, almost obscured the homegrown form of modernism known as the Chicago School, which had begun with Louis Sullivan and his marvelous new steel-framed skyscrapers of the late nineteenth century, and had continued into the twentieth century with Frank Lloyd Wright. Both branches of modernism would eventually find a receptive audience in California in the domestic architecture of Wright, Neutra, Richard M. Schindler, and Charles Eames.

California held its own exhibition devoted to the modern garden in San Francisco's Museum of Art, February to March, 1937. It was the first of three such shows, comprised largely of drawings, photos, and models, which demonstrated the interrelatedness of the modern house and garden. Along with Neutra, Schindler, and Church, it featured the work of architect William Wurster and landscape architects Geraldine Knight (Scott) and Lockwood de Forest.

This Altadena home illustrates the practical uses Eckbo applied to garden design, in blending house and garden, as well as capturing some of the natural aspects of the site.

In his introduction to the exhibition pamphlet, *Contemporary Landscape Architecture*, G.L. McCann Morley writes:

"At first the landscape architect was called in to soften the too strange and novel architecture with a garden that obscured rather than emphasized the style of the house. But the house "to live in" called for a garden "to live in" as an integral part of itself. Architects and landscape architects have begun to collaborate on the problem as a whole, with the result that not only is the house conceived for its function and its adaptation to the site, but the garden is also designed to harmonize with the house." [47]

In the same pamphlet, Henry-Russell Hitchcock, Jr. describes the integration of garden and house as being basic to the purpose of each: "However terraces are paved, with turf, or concrete slabs, or stone or brick or gravel, the larger part of their area should be open so that furniture may be freely grouped, as in an interior." [48]

The depression years, for all their hardship and deprivation, had provided the country—and particularly California—with the perfect crucible for experimentation. Citizens were eager for new ideas and challenges, in science and technology, government recovery programs, and—most of all—the arts. This was the world that was beckoning to Garrett Eckbo at Harvard in 1937.

Using the principles of design formulated by Gropius and the modern architects, as well as artists like Mondrian, Picasso, and especially Georges Braque, Eckbo defined modernism in terms of garden design, using the visual construction of the cubist painters and Gropius' approach to function. Perhaps more than architecture, cubism provided Eckbo with the bridge between geom-

Top: The original ERW partnership in 1948. From left to right: Garrett Eckbo, Francis Dean, Edward Williams, and Robert Royston. Dean became a full partner with Eckbo and Williams when Royston left in 1958.

etry and nature that had always been lacking in landscape architecture. While basing their works on nature, the cubists restated complex form in simpler, straight-forward planes, which added dimensions in movement and time by depicting several sides of a place or object simultaneously. The key to Cubism's mystique was often to be found in the use of diagonal lines or planes which invariably added dynamic force to a composition. A good example is Marcel Duchamp's *Nude Descending A Staircase*, 1911.

Using the diagonal to coalesce natural and geometric form and to provide tension, direction, and dynamic quality, Eckbo devised a new axiality, a new geometry without symmetry but with balanced structure in order and space. To this blending of natural and geometric form, Eckbo and the other modernists added visual rhythm to their garden composition, which consists primarily of repeated images in some regular—or expanding—order: a checkerboard grid with the squares changing from pavement to grass to groundcover, hexagonal variations with all of the garden elements forming units or multiples of units even as they change from lawn to

deck, seat wall to stepping stones. Fences, retaining walls and planters, overhead structures all serve to continue producing visual rhythm by means of repetitive structural and decorative elements, zig-zag planters and pulsating curvilinear walls. By the same means, this rhythmic cadence provides a garden with a sense of *scale*. We measure the basic unit—a brick, a square tile—in our mind's eye and multiply it subconsciously. In this way, a large courtyard or shopping mall is reduced to a single grid square from which we can subconsciously multiply it to its furthest dimensions and thereby construct a relationship in scale to ourselves. The courtyard or shopping mall may be huge, but the grid gives us a connection through which we can visually gain its measure.

Rhythm also provides an otherwise complex composition with order and discipline. The various elements of line and form engage logically. The pieces combine and enhance the whole. They do not compete or tend to unravel in strident discord. Some of the lessons found in the non-objective compositions of artists like Mondrian and Mark Rothko, as well as cubists Braque, Picasso, and Duchamp, are applicable to garden design.

Above: In this Eckbo garden, the interior opens out to the patio, the pool, and the distant vistas.

Opposite: Eckbo's Berkeley garden, with "scrap wood sculpture wall" that he designed and built (from a letter to the author).

In *Landscape For Living,* which Eckbo wrote in 1949 with the help of his partners Edward Williams and Robert Royston, he established a three-step process for landscape design: First, the designer must understand historic precedents in order to make use of their concepts while avoiding simplistic duplication. He reminds us that: "There never has been...a Spanish garden outside of Spain...an Italian Renaissance garden since the Italian Renaissance." [49]

This is more than simple disapproval of copying. Eckbo is here addressing an age old truth—original design is born out of the soil and time in which it was nurtured, underscoring the undeniability of *Iowa* in a Grant Wood painting, the midwest in Sinclair Lewis' *Main Street*, the New York in Cole Porter's '*Night And Day*,' the Miami Beach in *Streamline Moderne*. Eclecticism is most appropriate where ethnic and environmental similarities to the source occur, as Eckbo acknowledges:

"800 years of benevolent and productive autocracy of the Moors left marks on Spanish culture which no amount of physical destruction could erase. The typical 'Spanish' garden today throughout Latin America as well as the Iberian Peninsula, is the patio—enclosed, intimate, secluded." [50]

Second, the designer must develop an analytical process which can interpret the existing natural conditions (site analysis) and assess the stated project requirements (program). In the old Medi-

terranean Revival gardens, fragments and memorabilia of Andalusia and Tuscany were adapted to the southern California lifestyle and landscape. But in the modern garden, the design would evolve from the needs of the owners, the conditions of the site, and its orientation. Eckbo reminds us that democracy, as a behavioral determinant, "has been expressed in humanity of scale, simplicity and practicality in detail, and flexibility in plan conception." [51]

Third, the designer must establish a logical basis for form. The ancient Greeks derived it from the *golden mean*. The Renaissance architects Leone Battista Alberti and Andrea Palladio found models for form and proportion in nature and in musical harmony. In Eckbo's words: "Modern sculpture and painting have shown us how organically geometry emerges from nature, how all relations of forms in nature are subject to basic geometric analysis. Examination of rock books reveals the basic crystalline structure of many rocks to be straight-sided geometric forms." [52]

Above: Enclosure is softened when fencing allows for visual penetration in this Garrett Eckbo garden, Stone Canyon in Bel Air.

Middle: This Holmby Hills garden illustrates Eckbo's use of angular form to direct interest and movement.

Opposite: Fountain detail in a small Eckbo garden, Pacific Palisades.

Bottom: Aluminum overhead detail at Eckbo's home in Laurel Canyon (Wonderland Park), Los Angeles.

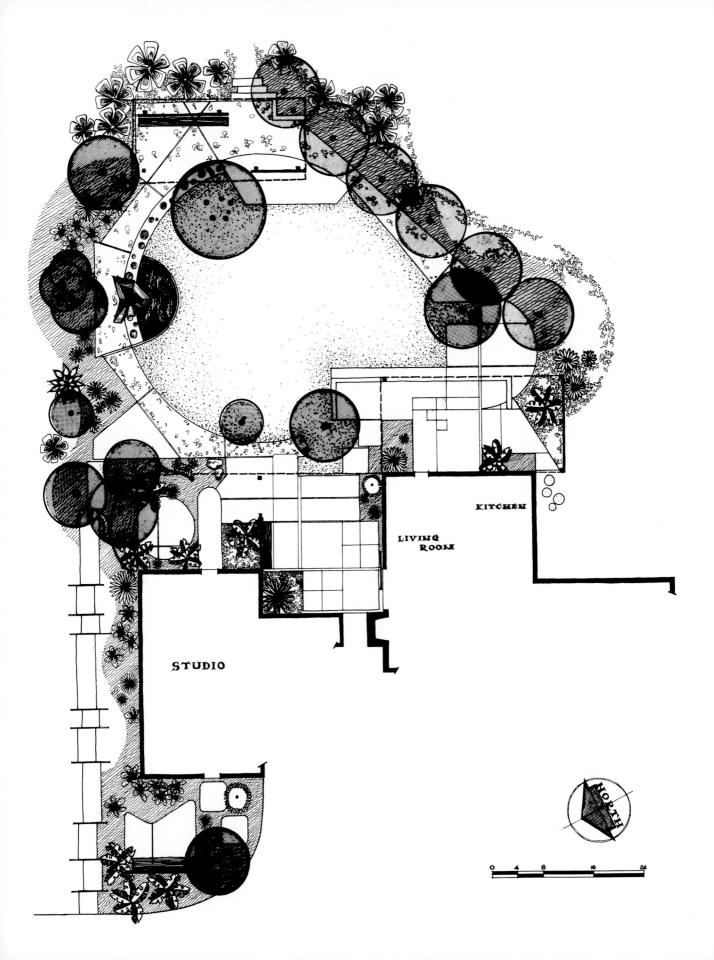

KITCHEN

LIVING
ROOM

STUDIO

NORTH

0   4   8   16   24

Eckbo's theories on modern design were similar to those held by Fletcher Steele, from an article dated December 1936, in *Contemporary Landscape Architecture*:

"18th century (garden designers) banished not only axial symmetry but every other sign of formal man-made design. Their effort was to follow the irregular, picturesque balance of natural scenery at its best...in no time the proponents of each school were tearing out each other's hair, for no particular reason that the really modern designer can understand. The two were kept strictly apart for 200 years."

"Now the effort is being made to harmonize the two by mixing formal and informal where common sense and true aesthetic satisfaction warrant. The combination is deliberate: a method of relieving the often monotonous stiffness of formal work and bringing manifest order into nature which in more cases than not, seems to express chaos rather than design...the old axis is retained in spirit, but changed almost beyond recognition. It is shattered and its fragments moved, duplicated and bent, as is the theoretical axis of any good natural scenery. Formal objects are put thus in occult rather than symmetrical balance." [53]

Opposite: Eckbo's plan for his Laurel Canyon garden.

Below: Arlene and Garrett Eckbo with workers building their Laurel Canyon garden, Los Angeles, 1959.

Twelve years later, at the post-war peak of the evolution of the modern garden in San Francisco, a second exhibit was held at the city's Museum of Art. In its guide, Eckbo presented his own views on the structure of the modern garden, concentrating on the role of plants. He concludes:

"To date most landscapers have tended to hide behind the thoughts that only-God-can-make-a-tree, that their primary materials are non-industrialized—and that, therefore, they needn't worry about 'modern design'. Materials should be used, developed, and handled so as to express and bring forth their own native qualities rather than be forced to fit certain arbitrary pre-conceptions as to form. They should serve a structural function in the solution of human living problems rather than be used in a decorative matter. Materials in landscape design should be used in the development of plans for the effective and creative organization of three-dimensional space." [54]

For his part, Church added commentary in the same 1948 guide expressing his contention that all of the available lot—front and rear—was garden and must be viewed as space for family activities, no longer simply "a place for shrubbery and flowers, and a place to hang the clothes." [55] By this time, the concept of the garden as a room—walled, aesthetically detailed, and multi-functional—was firmly established in San Francisco.

For a short time in 1938, Eckbo had worked for Thomas Church, but conflicts soon developed between their two rather headstrong personalities, and soon Eckbo left Church's employ to work for the Farm Securities Administration (1939-42), and the U.S. Housing Authority (1942-45). There, he gained respect for the courage and endurance of the migrant farm workers and dust bowl immigrants who were trying to scratch out a living in the San Joaquin Valley at that time. This was to be his first experience in multiple-housing planning, and the minuscule budget provided by the government added special challenges.

In 1945, with his brother-in-law Ed Williams and Robert Royston (both University of California graduates), Eckbo opened a practice of landscape architecture in downtown San Francisco. Two years later he departed for Los Angeles with Francis Dean to open a branch office there and to bring modern landscape design to southern California.

Garrett Eckbo's own garden in Laurel Canyon (Los Angeles), shows his experimentation with garden use of aluminum in cast fountain and extruded screens. The curved form of the garden connects, encloses, and unifies the various garden elements.

Douglas Baylis
and
Sunset Magazine

During the years following World War II, many California landscape architects added to the growing maturity of garden design. Douglas Baylis, Lawrence Halprin, and Theodore Osmundson are among the more successful men who had begun their careers working in the offices of Thomas Church or Eckbo, Royston and Williams. Baylis, who worked for Church from 1941-43, eventually opened an office in San Francisco, and following Church's example, kept it a small, personally controlled practice, largely aimed at residential design. His clients were generally of modest means, and Baylis's work became known for its efficiency of space and function.

In time, he came to realize that in order for the modern garden to become established within the middle income range of California home owners it would be necessary for him to publish his ideas. He therefore began writing a series of design articles for *Sunset Magazine* in 1951. The editor at that time, Walter Doty, completely restructured the magazine's approach, directing it toward the usefulness and flexibility of the modern garden, while directing it away from the ethereal flower-and-show character of most traditional garden magazines of the times. Baylis regularly contributed practical ideas and good design concepts for young homeowners, knowing that for many readers, hiring a landscape architect was not an option.

This self-help approach, fostered by Baylis and Doty, was to become the abiding philosophy of the magazine, and remains so today. Baylis' theoretical and practical contributions to the evolution of the modern California garden ended with his untimely death in 1971.

Above: Douglas Baylis, photographing a project near San Francisco, 1968.

Opposite Left: Owners of this steep San Francisco hillside garden were avid art collectors—Baylis used the site to display their collection of sculpture, 1953.

Opposite Bottom: Baylis uses canvas and galvinized pipe column to provide needed shade for this brick patio in Belvedere, 1948.

*Opposite top right and middle: Foothill Farms, near Sacramento. A 1956 tract development with five model home gardens by Doug Baylis, sponsored by **Better Homes and Gardens** magazine.*

Left: Sketch by Maggie Baylis of an enclosed garden was the model for the Drake patio. Maggie and Doug Baylis collaborated on a number of how-to pieces for **Sunset** *during the 1950s.*

Above: The 1947 studio garden for Gordon Drake, near Carmel, by landscape architect Douglas Baylis. View from interior to enclosed garden.

*Left: Baylis designed many small gardens in collaboration with **Sunset** magazine, like this series of enclosed spaces, to illustrate garden ideas for homeowners on a budget.*

Below: This 1950 Baylis garden, located in the hills above Oakland, was planned for maximum of family outdoor activities, as well as for views into the city below.

Opposite: Small hillside garden for a San Francisco architect. Baylis uses sand and brick-in-sand in a thirty degree grid pattern to articulate garden elements, 1958.

Post-War:
Housing
and
Population

Much of the technological evolution in war-driven industries eventually led to futuristic speculation and peacetime consumer-oriented production, from streamlined appliances to aviation-age housing.

Architects experimenting with steel, aluminum, and a variety of approaches to pre-fabricated structures developed units that could be mass produced in factories and erected on site in a few hours' time or air-lifted to hilly sites by means of helicopter. Glass canopies, products of the southern California aircraft industry, were envisioned as a method for enclosing the entire outdoor living area for total environmental control; to turn deserts into personalized oases wherein one could grow any plant desired, or to create any climate or for that matter, any season. The post-war years were chronicled in the rosiest terms of futuristic technological progress—and growth. And California was at the forefront of this brave, new world.

The population boom in California, which had stalled during the depression years, began to heat up again after the war as veterans of the Pacific theater, having trained in southern California, were eager to settle in the balmy, orange-scented land that had enchanted them. Aviation and other military-related industries that had helped to bring an end to depression and unemployment

in California were converted to peacetime production, providing jobs for returning servicemen. This time they came to stay, bringing wives, war brides and families to such unfamiliar places as Azusa, West Covina, and El Segundo.

The housing industry, dormant for nearly twenty years, sprang back into life, spewing formula-driven tracts of look-alike houses across the grassy hillsides and wooded valleys, over the bean fields, cattle ranches, and citrus orchards of Los Angeles and Orange Counties. By 1950, the rural face of southern California had been greatly altered, causing Eckbo to reflect:

"The majority of our population now lives in urban areas which have destroyed the natural primeval or rural environment and replaced it with the least, the shoddiest, and most mediocre of the American genius. We have abandoned the garden to find, not the potential Shangri-La...but anarchy, squalor, confusion, blight and slum." [56]

The loss of productive agricultural land during the post-war decade in California was without precedent. In 1947, for instance, Los Angeles and Orange Counties' citrus groves numbered over 135,000 acres of orange, lemon, and grapefruit trees, but by 1960, the total count was under 50,000. Most of the grapefruit and lemon growers started anew in the Coachella Valley and elsewhere—out of the path of the housing juggernaut—but oranges, the most

Opposite: In Palm Springs, industrial designer Raymond Loewy brings the desert into his structured oasis, pool into the living room, in this 1947 collaboration with architect Albert Fry.

lucrative product of the citrus industry, nearly disappeared from southern California. To a large degree, the loss of farmland has resulted from a shortsighted property tax system in the state which focused on potential land value rather than on actual use, forcing growers and ranchers to sell out to housing developers. (The California Land Conservation Act of 1965, also known as The Williamson Act, partially corrected this inequity.)

Eric Malnic, a reporter for the *Los Angeles Times*, recalls his youth in Azusa and the rapid changes that occurred there in the late 1940s:

"It was a typical southern California farm town in those days—mostly oranges, with a scattering of lemons, avocados and row crops...streets lined with palm, eucalyptus and pepper trees...sprawling farmhouses in the groves. The real excitement began about ten years later, when, as teen-agers, we watched in awe as bulldozers rooted out the orchards where we'd worked as farmhands and tore away the surrounding brushlands where we'd hunted jack-rabbits. The rural countryside we'd roamed so freely was soon replaced with asphalt parking lots, tacky shopping centers, and mean little houses so small that some of them were hauled in on the backs of flatbed trucks. Sure, it was ugly." [57]

But there seemed to be room for everyone who followed the disappearing scent of orange blossoms and the dream of owning a house of one's own, no matter how small. Never mind the unrecorded, unmentioned environmental havoc that was being carried out against wildlife and wilderness—in the name of growth.

Between 1930 and 1960, the population of the state tripled, with Orange County growing from 119,000 to over a million people in that time. Nationwide, the record of cheaply built, poorly planned mass housing development was similar, causing John Keats to write his devastating analysis in 1956, *The Crack In The Picture Window*: "For literally nothing down...you could find a box of your own in one of the fresh-air slums we're building around the edges of America's cities. There's room for all at any price range, for even as you read this

whole square miles of identical boxes are spreading like gangrene throughout New England, around Los Angeles, Chicago, Washington, Miami—everywhere." [58]

Outside San Francisco and Oakland in the Berkeley hills, the sprawl of look-alike houses inspired Malvina Reynolds in 1956 to write her famous put-down of California's housing industry:

*"Little boxes on the
hillside,
Little boxes made of
ticky tacky
Little boxes on
the hillside
Little boxes all the same
There's a pink one,
and a green one,
And a blue one,
and a yellow one,
And they're all made out
of ticky tacky,
and they all look just the
same."* [59]

Opposite Top: Richard Neutra brought modern architecture to Montecito in this exemplary 1947 house. Ralph Stevens contributed a picturesque water-conscious garden, bridging Mediterranean and modern eras in his long practice as a landscape architect. (also seen on next page)

Opposite Bottom: A post-war tract house, one of thousands built in Los Angeles and surrounding counties in 1947-50, illustrates ways to achieve outdoor living and a California lifestyle—on a budget. Sliding glass doors had not yet been introduced, but scored concrete and walled property lines were already in evidence.

Rapid post-war growth in the steep hillsides of Berkeley and Oakland vastly exceeded the earlier development there, which had begun in the late nineteenth century. The fires, which devastated the area in October of 1991, were probably heightened by the gradual replacement of most of the native trees in the area with highly volatile eucalyptus trees, brought in from Australia.

But despite this calamitous growth rate and the state's failure to manage it correctly, the 1950s were years of truly great innovation and imaginative design. Tragically though, very few of the post-war technological production methods envisioned by the futurists ever entered the mainstream of the Federal Housing Authority's development plans. Konrad Wachsman's Lego-like pre-fabricated structural system, which could be assembled on site by unskilled workmen in half a day; Rafael Soriano's erector-set steel framing and assembly line parts; John Lautner's clamshell posthouses, and a host of other building innovations were better-mouse-traps put on hold, while conventional stick-built housing flourished in California.

Among the latter builders were Eichler Homes who used several architects to achieve modern efficiency of space and architect-builder Cliff May who designed ranch-style tract homes on quarter of an acre lots. Although May preferred larger lots with existing trees and clients who owned horses, he also brought design efficiency to the budget housing market.

Thomas Church, Eckbo, Royston and Williams, Douglas Baylis, and other landscape architects of the post-war modern movement worked with Eichler and May to achieve a measure of quality living not found in earlier tract homes, which were usually clapboard boxes of 800 square feet with two tiny bedrooms, a kitchen and bath at the rear, a combination living room and dining area up front. Eichler, for one, reversed this configuration, putting the bedrooms up front and creating an entry that led to a living room at the rear, with a sliding glass door that gave way to a private garden and patio.

Architects like Wurster, Bernardi and Emmons (who did many upscale houses with Church) also contributed to improving the woefully sterile nature of tract house plans in the early post-war years.

Landscape architects, working at the outset of a housing project with the developer, the architect, and the more progressive local planning agencies, managed to enhance these small lots by using flexible zoning ordinances that allowed manipulation of side-yard requirements, enclosing rear walls, shorter front-yard setbacks, and corner lot walls and/or fences. Requirements for some minimal streetside landscaping, the planting of designated street trees, and the protection of existing mature trees helped to distinguish some of California's post-war housing tracts from the nightmare developments that John Keats had described.

Opposite: Ralph Stevens' garden in Montecito for a Richard Neutra house, 1947.

Lawrence Halprin: New Challenges in the Garden

The fourth major figure to emerge in California as a modernist intepreter of garden design was Lawrence Halprin. What the depression of the 1930s had done for Church, in terms of spurring him to establish a practical and economic approach to private garden design, the immediate postwar era had given Halprin the opportunity to forge social equity with design purpose. By chance, he arrived in San Francisco—his ship was sunk by a Japanese Kamikazi attack in the Pacific—and while recuperating there, he began to look for employment. After his discharge from the navy, he found work in the office of Thomas Church.

Born in Brooklyn in 1916, Halprin spent much of his youth roaming the wooded, semirural landscape near his home. Summer camp in Massachusetts further developed his love of nature, including his growing interest in sketching. Touring Europe's great gardens with his parents and a three year stint in a kibbutz in Israel helped to shape his eye for landscape design, as well as his lifelong concern for social welfare and justice. He studied horticulture at Cornell and subsequently began teaching that subject at the University of Wisconsin, where by chance, he came into contact with Frank Lloyd Wright at Taliesin. Impressed by Wright to become an architect, Halprin enrolled at Harvard under Walter Gropius, but after reading Christopher Tunnard's *Gardens In The Modern Landscape*, he recognized the career he had unknowingly been seeking since his summers of sketching in the wilds of Massachusetts. It was 1939, and the influence of modernism on American schools was at its peak. Along with Gropius, Tunnard, and Marcel Breuer, his instructors included Norman Newton, Walter Chambers, and Joseph Hudnut—and such classmates as future

Above: Lawrence Halprin at Sea Ranch, 1986

Opposite Bottom: An early modern garden by Halprin in downtown San Francisco. Bright colored plywood panels, raised redwood planters, and brick-on-sand were hallmarks of the San Francosco School of the late 1940s. Halprin describes the California garden as, "a simple garden for simple people. It broke away from Renaissance patterns, attitudes, and principals of design." (from a letter to the author).

giants of modernism Paul Rudolph, I.M. Pei, John Warnecke, and Philip Johnson. It was an electrifying environment for a young design student.

Tunnard, Gropius's landscape equivalent, had come to Harvard from Europe only a short time earlier, where he had designed a number of gardens based on the Bauhaus tenets of modernism. Spiritedly independent and imaginative, he published this credo of design:

"We believe in the probity of the creative act...the reliance of the designer on his own knowledge and experience, and not on the academic symbolism of the styles or outworn systems of aesthetics, to create new forms which are significant of the age from which they spring." [60]

Top: This architect's home illustrates best use of glass walls in modern design, providing views into the garden and beyond, to the sea. Lawrence Halprin.

Halprin's graduate era at Harvard, 1939-41, was his introduction to modernism through the teachings of Tunnard, Gropius, and the other design theorists with whom he came into contact there. For him, modern design was neither a reaction against classic or beaux arts principles, nor a rejection of existing standards in art and architecture. By this time, the artistic concepts introduced by Gropius had been largely accepted by east coast designers, and Church and Eckbo were back in San Francisco introducing the modern garden to California.

Halprin was familiar with the work of these two California landscape architects who had preceded him at Harvard, but Tunnard made the greater impression on his development as a designer. Like Gropius, Tunnard taught function, unencumbered by stylistic dogma or obligatory, formalized procedure. In *Gardens In The Modern Landscape,* he states:

"The plants, the paved surfaces, the seating, the focus just as in the Mies living room must also include the furniture, the flooring, the location of windows, the overall organization...the garden is planned in such a way as to form a direct relationship to the house, access from one to the other being everywhere facilitated...its arrangement is decided more for the activities of people...than for flowers." [61]

The garden interpreted as an outdoor room, a spatial sequence complete with enclosure, furniture, place and circulation, was certainly understood and pursued in California even before the modern era, but Tunnard can be credited with recognizing its similarities to architectural precepts—space and function—as conceived by Gropius and the Bauhaus designers. For Tunnard, the way to achieve dynamics in space and circulation in the garden was through asymmetric balance by breaking the rigid and static formality of bilateral symmetry that had dominated design throughout much of the Mediterranean revival. Eckbo had also seen the need to express implied movement in garden design,

managing it by use of diagonal projection and directing angles of 60 and 45 degrees. Eckbo's credo was a combining of ancient garden methods—the geometric and the natural. But for Tunnard, the modern garden was more a rejection altogether of the romanticized landscape: "(The landscape architect) is no longer bound by conventional imitation of picturesque nature as a long perpetrated artistic fraud. He shakes off the academic yoke of styles, free to interpret the message of his work of art in a new and more forceful manner." [62]

Opposite: A roof garden by Halprin, overlooking the San Francisco Bay.

This Page: The Halprins' home in Marin County. Every effort was made to preserve the natural integrity of the site. House and garden grow out of the structure of the topography.

During his four-year tenure with Church, 1946-1950, Halprin designed practical and inexpensive gardens for tract houses. On occasion, opportunities of some magnitude would come into the office, and one of these was from a Sonoma farmer, Dewey Donnell, who wanted to add a pool and poolhouse as a kind of retreat to his farmhouse. Church did most of the preparatory work himself and left Halprin with the responsibility of carrying the scheme into final form. It was to become the most significant single residential garden project of their combined talents.

Halprin dismisses any references to direct influence on his work from paintings and other art forms of the modern movement: "People have called the Donnell garden cubistic, but I don't see it. The forms came more from nature, the surrounding landscape, than from abstract art." [63] Yet he allows that some free expression represented in the works of Joan Miro and Wassily Kandinsky might also result from the same kind of search for form which eventually evolved into the splendidly interactive curvilinear pool, lawn, and concrete deck of the Donnell garden (see pages 208-209).

For Halprin, the garden represented a challenge to create a new art form which was artistic in its aesthetic structure while being responsible to its purposes and human needs. The garden was not in any way a decorative art to him; rather, the garden was a total structure whose decorative merit could only be interpreted within its overall form, and the degree to which it met its clients' wishes. Without realizing it perhaps, he was restating the argument made for modern art by Piet Mondrian years before, whereby form is reduced to its essential elements of universal and utopian expression. The Donnell garden ideally expresses this concept.

In California, Halprin found a ready canvas for interpreting the design theories of Tunnard and Gropius—purity of form and totality of function. He considered it to have been his good fortune that World War II dumped him, literally, in San Francisco Bay; for it was here that he found the chance to fully articulate Tunnard's philosophy.

Halprin lists four qualities that he believes have affected the development of the modern California garden as separate from garden form elsewhere: the *climate* as a factor in designing for year-round use, the public's *lack of preconceived notions* regarding form or style in contemporary garden design, the *Spanish heritage* which has always given the patio a central role in the household, and finally the concept of *edge*.

Opposite: Plan and overview of this small San Francisco garden by Lawrence Halprin. Garden structure separates outdoor living areas from storage and vegetable plots. Says Halprin, "Transitions and edges became important as a way to overcome climate and topography problems through design. The architecture and micro-architecture echoed these transitions by separating pieces of the house. Unlike the Japanese garden, (the California gardens) were not only visual but also functional, providing service yards, playgrounds, vegetable gardens." (from a letter to the author).

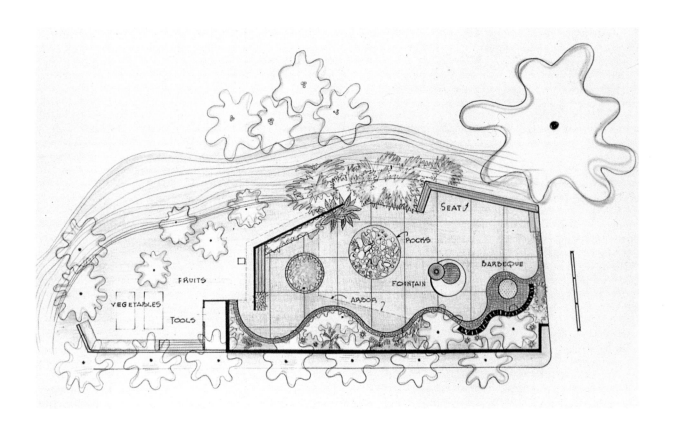

According to Halprin, the gardens of more temperate climates may be more readily adapted to blending with natural forms, and the separation between what is natural and what is manufactured may become blurred. But in California, this division needs to be more strongly delineated—a result of an arid climate and less hospitable plant species and communities in nature, resulting in the introduction of many exotic plants, fire protection, irrigation systems, and a somewhat altered growing season—all of which tend to create *edge*.

Halprin nevertheless remains aware of nature's role in the California garden. For him, the modern garden became a practical way of responding to the needs of California families in the post-war era who chose to leave the city in favor of tract house living:

"Forty years ago Tommy and I were doing drought-tolerant residential gardens. It was not a new concept for us. And we didn't fight the topography but let it work for us, by using lots of wood decks to ease the need for massive grading, cut and fill, retaining walls." [64]

During the late 1940s and early 1950s, Halprin continued to concentrate his practice in the design of residential gardens, from the early 800 square-foot boxes on one-quarter acre lots (costing about $6,500 at that time), to the large estates of the wealthy, and the experimental designs of avant-garde architects and their artistic clients. Occasionally experimenting himself, he tried his hand at writing, film-making, explorative theatre, and administrative therapy, but he always came back to landscape architecture and garden designing in particular. The garden would remain his crucible for design experimentation, as demonstrated in such recent projects as the Franklin Delano Roosevelt Memorial Garden in Washington, D.C. and the stairway that connects the Los Angeles Public Library to Bunker Hill. "Most of the folks that I had for clients didn't want a garden as such," he noted, "they wanted a beautiful piece of sculpture to live in." [65] Stephen C. Pepper, Professor of philosophy and chairman of the art department at the University of California, Berkeley, underscored this concept in a 1948 paper, *The Introduction to Garden Design*, stating:

"Recently, painting, sculpture and architecture have been rediscovering space. It may come as a surprise to learn that landscape architecture has been doing the same. After passing through its periods of imitation of nature and of reminiscent treatment of styles of other epochs, this art, like the others, has discovered the immediate delights in the plastic treatment of space. The creation of a garden in this new light becomes something half way between the making of a painting and the making of a house. It is as if the landscape architect were composing an abstract painting for people to live in." [66]

California's historic gardens, the rancho patio and Mediterranean revival, clearly established the garden as both functional and spatial. The modern garden, however, while following that tradition with ever increasing efficiency, surprise, and originality, has raised garden design to new levels of artistic quality. Indeed, a piece of sculpture. Pepper goes on:

"A garden is no longer essentially a visual prospect from a window or balcony, or summer house...it is practically part of the house. And yet at the same time it shares something of the spontaneity and freedom of imagina-

tive spatial composition characteristic of painting—particularly of abstract painting. The fact that bricks and concrete and wood and glass become garden materials often occupying much more space than flowers and shrubs should not disturb us." [67]

During the 1950s, the modern movement in California reached its zenith and began moving south. A number of imaginative young architects in California began to interpret modernism in ways especially suited to the climate and topography of Los Angeles, using open interior plans, wide expanses of floor-to-ceiling glass, and broad overhangs to keep the sun from reaching these glass curtain walls. Pierre Koenig, Craig Ellwood, Robert Alexander, Gregory Ain and John Lautner were on the vanguard of southern California's rush to redefine

the earlier efforts of William Wurster and Cliff May. Charles Eames, who came to California in the war years to design studio sets, exemplified the entire movement by applying new materials and technology to architecture, furniture design, and machinery. Others, like Richard Nuetra and industrial designer Raymond Loewy, proved equally versatile and inventive, as were they all.

Above: A Halprin garden in San Francisco for an admiral shows patio enclosed by wings of the house, and good indoor-outdoor transition.

181

Garrett Eckbo, who had opened a new office of Eckbo, Royston and Williams in Los Angeles in 1946, had correctly timed his arrival in the south to take advantage of the arrival of modernism there. Until this time, both house and garden, still rooted in Mediterranean revival, had lagged behind in southern California. Acting more or less as a vanguard for modernism, Eckbo pioneered the modern garden in the south, a distinction he shared with Francis Dean, who was to become his new partner (along with Edward Williams) after Robert Royston left the San Francisco office in 1958.

Following his military service in World War II, Dean entered the University of California, Berkeley, in 1945 to study landscape architecture under Leland Vaughan. While there, he became acquainted with Robert Royston and the gardens designed in the San Francisco area by Thomas Church and the new firm of Eckbo, Royston and Williams:

"My fondest wish was to be able to design gardens such as [theirs]—I thought they were magnificent. In addition, several of us would take trips on the weekends just to visit their gardens that were under construction and try to understand the concepts behind what we saw developing on the ground. At the time, of course, I had no idea that I would someday have the opportunity and pleasure of working on some of those great gardens with Garrett Eckbo during the '50s and '60s." [68]

In San Francisco, Williams continued to maintain the practice there after 1958, now under the name of Eckbo, Dean and Williams, and Royston opened a new practice with two staff members, Asa Hanamoto and David Mayes as his partners. Royston, Hanamoto and Mayes soon became one of the most successful and influential landscape architectural firms in the nation.

Tree trunk and foliage patterns dominate this Lawrence Halprin garden in Marin County, about 1950.

Robert Royston: Teacher and Designer

Robert Royston also studied landscape architecture at the University of California, Berkeley, and after military service he returned to San Francisco in 1945 to join Eckbo and Williams. While working in the partnership from a downtown office building, he also taught landscape architecture at Berkeley, and later, on a part-time basis, taught at North Carolina State University, as well as several other design schools. During his own student days before the war, he had benefitted from the teachings of Thomas Church (by whom he was also employed), and was determined to continue in his professional career as both teacher and practitioner. With the organization of his own firm in 1958, this dual role became easier to manage. Royston's practice with his new partners grew rapidly in scope and range of projects, but private garden design remained its cornerstone over the years.

A painter and broad experimenter in both ideas and form, Royston, of all the early practitioners of the modern garden, was probably the most technically adroit garden designer to emerge from the San Francisco school. As a result, no doubt, of having kept a foot in both the academic and practical worlds of design, he searched for a deeper understanding of the relevance between form and use, and people's perceptions of the aesthetic versus the practical in garden design:

"There is almost always an overlap of professions, sometimes deliberately; the garden might find its roots in the structural unit of measure, 'the module,' or painting, or sculpture, or nature itself...my own explorations were stimulated by good works here and there: Kepes, Goldfinger, Eckbo, Greenough, Klee, Sullivan, Corbu, Mies, Roth, Matisse, Hasdorf—the list goes on and on—and I never forget Mother Nature." [69]

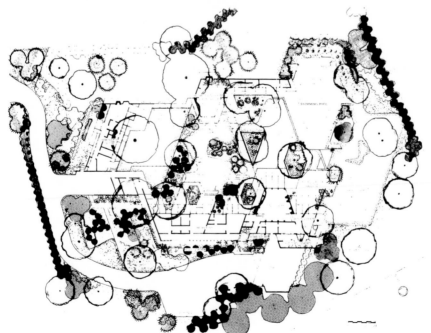

This spectacular site in Woodside provided Robert Royston with an opportunity to project angular unity throughout this late 1960s garden, in collaboration with architect Henry Hill.

Opposite Top: Robert Royston at his Mill Valley office in 1982.

Opposite Below: A Marin County Royston garden.

Opposite top: A Marin County garden by RHAA illustrating privacy and intimacy at both entry and poolside.

Opposite bottom: From this raised deck, one can view the swimming pool, or turn around to the enclosing wilderness, near Piedmont. Royston, Hanamoto, Abey and Alley, landscape architects.

Above: Royston's residence in Mill Valley, illustrating his garden deck which serves also as a bridge connecting the house to the studio at the foot of the garden.

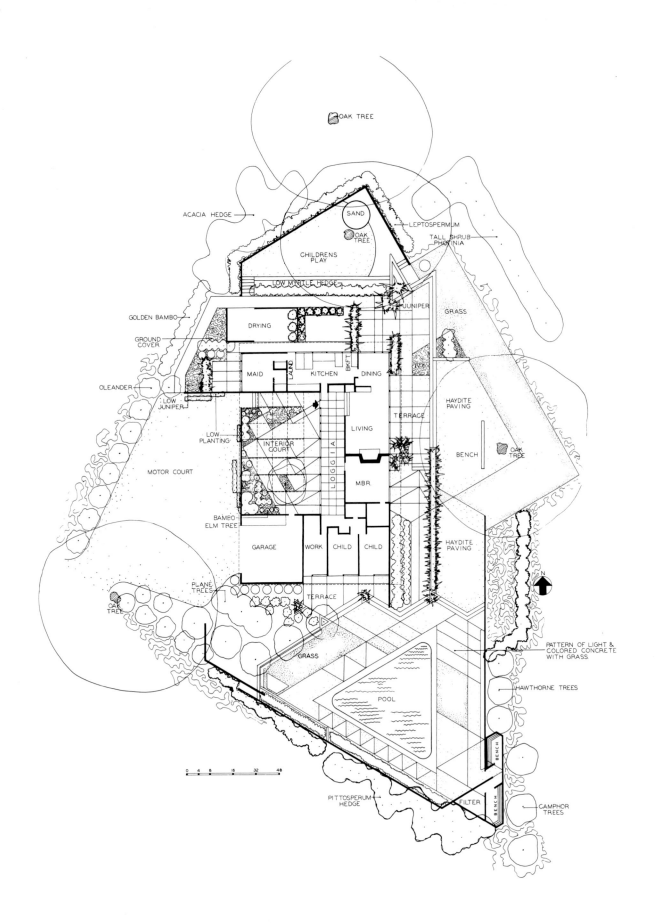

OAK TREE

ACACIA HEDGE

LEPTOSPERMUM

SAND

OAK TREE

TALL SHRUB PHOTINIA

CHILDRENS PLAY

LOW MYRTLE HEDGE

JUNIPER

GRASS

GOLDEN BAMBO

DRYING

GROUND COVER

MAID

LAUD

KITCHEN

BKFT

DINING

HAYDITE PAVING

OLEANDER

LOW JUNIPER

TERRACE

LOW PLANTING

INTERIOR COURT

L O G G I A

LIVING

BENCH

OAK TREE

MOTOR COURT

MBR

BAMBO ELM TREE

GARAGE

WORK

CHILD

CHILD

HAYDITE PAVING

PLANE TREES

N

OAK TREE

TERRACE

PATTERN OF LIGHT & COLORED CONCRETE WITH GRASS

GRASS

HAWTHORNE TREES

POOL

BENCH

0 4 8   16   32   48

PITTOSPERUM HEDGE

BENCH

FILTER

CAMPHOR TREES

Japanese Influences

The shape, character, and usefulness of the modern California garden that was evolving during the 1950s was also influenced by Japanese garden tradition. Having a climate similar to California's northern coast, Japan developed a garden ethic over several centuries that was not unlike the Moorish tradition of emphasizing privacy and intimacy of space through use of enclosing devices, as well as maintaining a close relationship between house and garden. The Japanese garden, however, makes a much stronger commitment to a connection with nature—symbolic or real—which limits its use to purposes more passive, contemplative, and visual in nature.

Lawrence Halprin was influenced by the Japanese garden, clearly understanding its values:

"Japanese gardens do not function, they are completely visual. They are not ways to expand the house or provide for recreation, but rather to encapsulate nature and give beautiful vistas." [70]

A closer look at the traditional Japanese garden reveals the following characteristics, some of which were certainly used by California's modernist landscape architects:

A *minimal* approach to design—reducing basics of form to simple geometry or purpose, with a bare minimum of plants and other materials.

An emphasis on *emotional values*—reflective, intuitive, meditative, peaceful, sacred.

Attention to *detail*—making the most of connectors, fastenings, change of material, and care in pruning and shaping of plants.

A recognition of the role of *nature in* the design of the garden, symbolizing natural events such as seasons, weather, streams, and movement.

A consideration for *composition*—recognizing the value of location, for viewing, gathering, contemplating, and creating elements of surprise, continuity, and extension.

A concern for *lineal progression*—making connections by directing the eye through a series of visual transitions within and even beyond the immediate garden.

One experiences a Japanese garden by walking through it, seeing it unfold along a pathway that provides interior events while projecting exterior views, always leading, coaxing one on around the weeping pine bough toward the next vista. In varying degrees, these characteristics may also be found in the modern California garden. When the design of the modern garden is viewed as *process,* combining both the natural and humanly contrived ingredients into a coordinated whole, Thomas Church's definition of modernism becomes clearer: a broad highway indeed.

Opposite: Another example of Royston's finesse in the use of angular form.

Another early modernist who was shaped in part by the work of Church and the other designers from the San Francisco connection was Theodore Osmundson who opened an office in the Bay Area with two friends, after having spent a short time in the Church office. Known for years as Osmundson and Staley, this practice grew from a residential scale into one of great range and variety of projects, most noteworthy being a series of roof gardens for corporations in and around the Bay area.

These are the designers who created the modern California garden. Church was the initial experimenter, the pragmatist and empiricist who searched for new forms to meet changing needs. Eckbo codified these efforts, explained and justified the new method in academic thought and language and carried experimentation even further. Royston provided stability of structure, a logic to its form, a clarity of organization and technique. Baylis popularized the modern garden through *Sunset* and other home magazines, and he gave it a cachet of desirability and a broader availability, helping to make the modern garden a singular California institution. Halprin raised the form to a level beyond the realm of one's own private world, and continued to experiment with shape and materials until the garden had achieved a place in the history of garden design alongside the Italian Renaissance, the French Formal, the Islamic, the English Natural, and the Japanese gardens. As such, it is the only truly new concept in garden art to have evolved in the United States.

Although a number of talented landscape architects followed in the footsteps of these San Francisco school pioneers, the modern movement in garden design had reached its apogee by 1960 and would soon be seen to wane in emphasis or give way to other needs. The great decade of design for its own sake was ending, and such things as social, economic, and political causes began to draw the attention of landscape architects and the public.

Below Ted Osmundson in Hawaii, 1978, and above, with Fred Stresau F.A.S.L.A., in Ft. Lauderdale, October 1967.

Opposite Page: Kaiser roof garden, Oakland, by Theodore Osmundson and Associates, 1960 (top). 1989 roof garden for Thoreau Hall, University of California at Davis, by Osmundson and Associates, landscape architects (bottom).

Population and Planning

During the 1960s, a measure of stability began to enter the runaway housing markets of both the Bay Area and southern California, largely through the efforts of local planning agencies which struggled to develop ordinances for achieving some degree of order in community development and through the private sector—architects, planners, landscape architects—who sought to correct some of the mistakes of the past by use of more precise and inclusive master planning. Some of the early attempts in the decade to achieve order and control in broad new housing projects and in the rapidly expansive nature of growth in metropolitan Los Angeles are described in *Los Angeles, The Ultimate City* (1965) by Christopher Rand. According to Rand, the citrus industry, economic anchor of southern California for nearly a century, had by 1965 all but disappeared under a tidal wave of bulldozing. The interurban transit system (the red cars), which had long served to connect the far-flung suburbs and semirural communities of the greater metropolitan area, had been scrapped for an ever-expanding freeway system, and air pollution, thought to have been a mixture of smoke and fog alone in those naive times, had by 1960 begun to cloak the once-blue skies overhead in an eye-irritating brownish shroud.

By 1965, California had passed New York as the most populous state in the nation, and planners in Sacramento, as well as Los Angeles, were beginning to use terms like *carrying capacity* and *growth parameters* as part of the lingo linked to a search for some semblance of growth control. The Southern California Association of Governments (SCAG) came into existence to provide new methods for trying to deal with the multi-faceted problems arising from an expanding and increasingly mobile population, where living in one community while commuting to another—a drive of maybe 50 to 100 miles each way—was no longer even considered particularly unusual.

Another answer was found in master planning. William Pereira (Pereira and Luckman), reacting to the many alarms warning of imminent disasters from further urban sprawl, developed an approach to structuring long-range planning programs that would address all the basic requirements of community living—housing, transportation, schools, protection, regulation, consumer needs, services, open space, recreation, and even employment. Housing was to be de-stratified (following a number of post-war studies by sociologists) and made available in a range of size and pricing tiers. In cooperation with progressive local planning agencies, the New Look for master-planned communities of the 1960s was to include such innovations as: *zero lot lines* (which would save side yard space for better use), the *Quimby Act* (which would pool such saved footage for use in the making of small neighborhood parks and play areas), *planned unit development* (which would encourage a pre-conceived mixing of housing types, from single family detached to town houses and high-rise apartment towers), *cluster housing* (which would offer a combination of private and shared neighborhood gardens and recreation areas), and *condominiums* (a new approach to the 1920s courtyard complexes).

Pereira and other planning futurists thought to eliminate the shortsighted hodge-podge of "checkerboard development" (a random selection of property for upcoming housing projects based on land cost and availability) and "rice paddy" hillside development (structuring the topography to meet the shape of the house—and the entire housing project—rather than the reverse). In Pereira's view, the future of metropolitan development in California would necessarily be found in long-range, rationally conceived planning projects—not unlike the post-war New Towns of Britain and Europe—that would be completely packaged to leave little chance for dullness and stratification—the curse of earlier, superficially planned post-war communities. Another result of "total planning," however, was the general disappearance of any element of the intuitive process, either at the outset of the project or during its evolution from drawing board to realized human community. Along with the normal city ordinances came designer "regulations and requirements" and carefully controlled locations for present and future amenities. The age of computer-driven design had arrived.

Master planning was not a new concept, however. It dated from the planned communities and new towns of the sixteenth-century Renaissance and more recently from the modern planning schemes of Le Corbusier, whose *Machine For Living* was a concept of efficiency in space and movement far beyond the imagination of most of us (or the willingness of most of us to imagine such a community). In California, as stated in the previous chapter, Frederick Law Olmsted and other designers had created the marvelously successful Palos Verdes Estates in the late 1920s, which included individually designed houses (with community covenants), parks, libraries, schools, commercial centers, and recreational opportunities. In 1940, architects Alexander and Johnson, with landscape architect Fred Barlow, Jr., had designed Baldwin Hills Village (now The Village Green), which became the forerunner for the best in condominium designs of the 1960s. Baldwin Hills Village was modeled on previous housing designs by Clarence Stein and Henry Wright, which were in their turn based on earlier concepts of British planner Raymond Unwin and before him Ebeneezer Howard, who developed the first approach to modern community planning at the end of the nineteenth-century. By classically simple logic, Alexander and Johnson had been able to more than triple the density of traditional single-family detached housing by eliminating lot lines, combining service and parking areas, and turning the houses to face an open greensward instead of the street. In this way, they could provide residents with a large, open area as well as smaller, individually owned patio gardens.

But the challenge of planning community living in the 1960s was more precise and exacting, more controlled, and Pereira was obliged to plan for complex and variable development, as well as to attempt to plot the future needs and growth patterns of a rapidly growing and more mobile society. The project which presented itself, on a scale far beyond any predecessor, was the 87,000 acre Irvine Ranch in southern Orange County. This would include housing of every kind, commercial centers of regional and neighborhood scale, a system of public parks, beaches and other recreational facilities, open space and agricultural areas—and a brand new University of California campus to provide the new city with instant presence. To achieve the goals of this large and diverse undertaking, Pereira and The Irvine Company employed many architects and planners, landscape architects, engineers, and other strategists with instructions to be as imaginative and creative as ongoing business practices would allow. In this way, Irvine pioneered condominium housing, planned unit development, and cluster housing, staying with innovative planning projects even when the market for such turned sluggish.

In the mid-1960s, Irvine was considered to be ahead of its times, but in those heady years of unspoiled growth, little thought was given to the effects all that massive construction must have been having on the environment. In the 1960s, the planners' term "unimproved land" was still the accepted official way of describing the natural landscape. Any expressed effort to protect our California wilderness, wildlife, natural habitat, scenic rivers, lagoons, and coastal estuaries was still a decade or more away—at least in terms of official concern.

The impetus for a change in the direction of landscape architects during the 1960s came largely from sociological pressures—the campaign for civil rights and voter registration in the south, anti-war sentiment throughout the nation, and a changing value structure in American society. To this end, landscape architects became involved in helping to provide for the open space and recreational needs of poor, underprivileged, and handicapped Californians. The 1960s were concerned not so much with protecting and improving the environment as with protecting and improving the status of people. Of course, the two are not mutually exclusive. Sociologists and environmentalists in later decades came to recognize the two issues as part of the same overriding concern: the health, safety, and happiness of humankind within a fully integrated and functioning natural environment. Although social welfare may have taken precedence over nature in the 1960s, making it the great decade of reform as well as anxiety, concern for the preservation of natural habitat and for design methods based on the rhythms of nature was already in evidence by this time. Landscape architects involved in contemporary housing projects began to reject the standards of postwar earth moving technology which so obliterated natural configuration, drainage systems, and existing plant and animal life, and to search for new methods, new processes of design that would insure nature's role in form giving while continuing to seek solutions that were in harmony with social progress. A model for such a combination of goals was established on the coast north of San Francisco. It was called Sea Ranch.

Al Boeke, owner of the property, came to Lawrence Halprin for help. Here, according to Halprin, was an opportunity that finally brought together the goals that he had been preparing himself to meet all of his life. In that wild, windswept stretch of north coast bluff, he saw the end product of his childhood years of sketching in the woods of New England, his teenage years in learning about community organization in an Israeli kibbutz, his preparation in modern landscape design from Church and Tunnard. With Charles Moore and other far-sighted architects of the era, he produced a community harmonious to the natural setting and likewise harmonious in its human relationships. Indeed, not only the structures, roads, grading, and planting were obliged to conform to the natural surroundings, but also, the very life-style of the inhabitants was expected to come into harmony with the rhythm of this spectacular site. It is the kind of place, the kind of natural environment where one is kept constantly in tune with the sound and feel of the place—the cool, moist ocean air, the variations in the calls of different gull species, the varying stages of life in the lichens that cling to the crevices in the outcrop. The people who live in Sea Ranch are sensitive to the changes in the wind, the migration of birds following the Pacific flyway, the time of bloom for coastal wildflowers. Their houses have the squat, enduring look of a North Sea village inhabited by fishing and seafaring folk. Of course, strict covenants limit owners' penchant for individual expression, and for that matter all man-made or otherwise unnecessary structural intrusions onto this pristine landscape are kept to a minimum, including paved surfaces, signs, lighting standards, power equipment, and service conduits.

Today, one passes Sea Ranch on State Highway One with a fair chance of missing it altogether, its weathered, windward sloping roof lines huddling beneath dark Monterey Cypress or half hidden behind wavery thatches of seagrass. Perhaps the only notable failure of Sea Ranch has been its inability to attract copiers. More likely, as with Baldwin Hills Village and Palos Verdes Estates, it failed to attract the mass-market developers, and like them is destined to remain an anomaly of imaginative design—outside Eckbo's view of the usual "anarchy, squalor, confusion, blight and slum." [71]

Above: Sea Ranch, on the Pacific coast above San Francisco. Architecture by Charles Moore, overall planning and landscape design by Lawrence Halprin.

Left: Sea Ranch home of Ann and Lawrence Halprin.

Mannerism in the Modern Garden

Garden design during the 1960s continued to evolve in the modern tradition of Church and Eckbo, but with some noticeable signs of regression—to earlier styles and devices. Asymmetric geometry remained the dominant theme, with even greater dependance on the inherent flexibility of forty-five degree and sixty-five degree corners as replacement for the older, simpler rectangular forms. Although Church, Eckbo, and Royston pioneered the use of hexagonal design, most landscape architects of the 1960s had discovered its versatility and were using it in a wide range of projects, in a variety of patterns and methods.

Materials used in the 1960s were also more varied, and construction techniques more elaborate, sophisticated—and more expensive. While the typical tract-house garden of the previous decade had been made to seem sparse, sharply defined, even severe in the use of pipe column-posts, rakishly angled eggcrate overhead structures, brightly painted fences with abstract sculpture mounted here and there, and metal-dish fountains fashioned from surplus industrial tanks, the sixties garden was less experimental, more staid in its concept and execution.

The 1960s garden used less concrete, even as exposed aggregate, in favor of older, more natural surfaces like tile, brick, and (unfortunately) grass. Fences of unpainted redwood gained favor as redwood itself grew scarce, and the glossy primary surfaces of the forties and fifties—plywood, aluminum, industrial plastics—gave way to mellow earth tones, in furnishings as well as in details and surface treatments. The concrete industry could not keep up with the demand for mud-colored block walls, and when at last the market seemed saturated, they switched to slumpstone—a mass-produced concrete block that was supposed to resemble adobe. Even canvas, rarely seen in garden usage after the 1930s, returned in an improved synthetic form which could readily stand up to salt air and California sunshine. The garden materials of the 1960s had begun to resemble their forebears of the Mediterranean revival.

The use of plant material in the 1950s garden had been directed toward achieving striking effect—a single, almost sculptural Bird of Paradise, Draco, or Japanese black pine emerging from between polished black stones, against a backdrop of brightly painted plywood paneling. Well-modulated and carefully underplanted schemes with aggregate or alternately colored paving patterns gave way to 1960s gardens that tended to be more fluffed-up, shrubbery replacing intricate fencing design for screening or to carry a visual line, as well as to soften the geometry of the house itself.

At the same time, the California housing market underwent similar changes which resulted in the gradual softening of modern residential architecture. Earth tones replaced the sharp white outline of the typical 1950s cubes, and further softening through use of exposed wood detailing changed the modern house to something less exciting, but probably more acceptable to public taste. The decade also saw the wholesale introduction of the swimming pool and spa—so common to California suburbia as to become cliches and objects of ridicule by television comedians. The redwood tub, which gave way to the more refined fiberglass spa, first became popular at Big Sur's natural hot springs in the early 1960s, and eventually found its way into many a private garden during the decade, complete with water heater, seating, and a host of hedonistic paraphernalia. By 1980, swimming pools had lost much of their earlier appeal, owing largely to an increase in the cost of maintenance and the amount of space taken up for them in ever-shrinking lot sizes. However, the tub and spa business continued to hold its own.

For the most part, Californians remember the 1960s as a decade of social reform, especially on the campuses and inner cities. The Vietnam War, riots in Los Angeles, and student uprisings at Berkeley were primary elements of the era, marked by popular reaction against long-established cold-war institutions and values. Landscape architects found themselves involved in social and political controversies that included questions of land ethic. The People's Park movement in Berkeley, attempts to protect the Redwood National Park through legislation, and the referendum to establish the statewide Coastal Commission to oversee beaches and coastline as a protection against unchecked development are memorable examples. Concern for the alarming rate of loss of historic buildings brought about the organization of preservation minded groups which soon turned attention, with the help of landscape architects, to the preservation of historic parks and other places.

Left: Jacuzzi detail— private residence in Buena Park. Landscape architects— Land Concern.

Opposite: Hillside garden near San Diego, by Richard Wilson, landscape architect.

The Garden Designers

During the decade of the 1960s, landscape architects who made progress in urban park design, open space planning, and the protection of historic places also continued to expand and explore the elements of the modern garden. Among the leading figures were Mai and David Arbegast, Don Brinkerhoff (Armstrong, Sharfman and Brinkerhoff), Morgan Evans, Jacques Hahn (Hahn and Hoffman), Richard Jones and Robert Peterson, Fred Lang and Kenneth Wood, Joseph Linesch, Michael Painter, Tito Patri, Courtland Paul, Owen Peters and Robert Erikkson (Balwin, Erikkson and Peters, later Erikkson, Peters and Thoms), Richard Taylor, Peter Walker (Sasaki and Walker), Emmet Wemple, Joe Yamada (Wimmer and Yamada), and others who carried the modern garden to new levels of beauty and usefulness.

These second-wave modernists came into garden design through a variety of entries. Emmet Wemple entered the University of Southern California with the idea of taking every course that interested him, nevermind majoring in something. More by chance than design, he picked up enough credits for a degree in fine arts, having become attracted to furniture making. He returned three years later, in 1951, to teach drawing and there met Garrett Eckbo, who had accepted a part-time position to train architects in the fine points of landscape design. For Wemple, the search to find a career for himself was now realized. Not only had he discovered landscape architecture as a new art form, but through Eckbo, he became exposed to the modern garden—just at the time that *Landscape For Living* was gaining a readership.

Above: A garden in Santa Monica—classic, simple elegance in modern formalism, by Emmet Wemple.

Pictured clockwise: Owen Peters, Courtland Paul, at the Peridian office, 1984; Donald Brinkerhoff; Emmet Wemple with early partner Bill Leone (right), 1954; Joseph Yamada and Harriett Wimmer in San Diego, 1969—two years after her retirement from active practice.

Through this exposure, he was quick to grasp Eckbo's concepts of garden as space, and the application of the book's lessons to southern California:

"We knew of the great English garden makers and those early landscape architects of the east, but we saw our place in southern California as unique...our clients were young families beginning their lives in southern California, who were enthusiastic with their house and garden....Active spaces, passive spaces, recreation, family activities were the terms considered." [72]

Like Royston and Eckbo, Wemple continued to teach while developing a practice in landscape architecture. His early training as a painter and furniture designer sharpened his instincts for precisely detailed gardens, and his broad academic background provided him with a passion for all that was poetic, lyrical, and roman-

tic in garden design. His esoteric side was balanced by the pragmatics of on-the-job problem solving: "We poured concrete, set brick in sand, and engineered walls and patio structures....In the academic world the emphasis is on theory, but in the profession the reality of synthesis becomes critical." [73] The Getty Museum garden in Malibu remains one of his favorite projects.

Below: Revived use of pre-cast concrete pavers in a revisited Mediterranean house and garden by Emmet Wemple.

Opposite: This 1970s garden in Brentwood by Wemple reflects the style of modern Mexican architecture.

Courtland Paul began his career in landscape architecture much like A.E. Hanson. Born and raised in Pasadena, he combined an early love of plants, sketching, and gardening for family and friends, leading to summer jobs with a local nursery where he was fortunate enough to come into contact with the installation of several Thomas Church gardens. For the young student, it was the beginning of a career and a life-long admiration for Church: "My principal influence was Tommy. I had worked on projects of his when I was with Bamico (Nursery). I learned a lot this way, like a sponge I soaked it up." [74]

After studying horticulture at Cal Poly, Pomona, he left to start a design-build business with two friends from the nursery, and in a very short time they had too much business to continue with the con-

Top left: The Ritz Carlton, Laguna Niguel. Designed by Peridian, Arthur G. Beggs.

Top right: Ted Osmundson and Courtland Paul at Yosemite National Park, about 1959.

Opposite: This Newport Beach garden design takes advantage of the 30 foot elevation change from the front street to the rear property line. Cascading waterfalls mitigate traffic noises from the busy streets below. Designed by Peridian, Courtland Paul

struction element. During the 1960s, with new partner Arthur Beggs, Paul became one of the most successful landscape architects in California, eventually re-shaping the partnership into a corporation, entitled Peridian. Like Church, he made close friends of his clients, returning to design new gardens for them as they moved from place to place: "It was always my intent," he said, "to create a little piece of paradise, a little corner of that person's world." [75] In keeping with the shifting tides of modernism, Paul's private gardens tend to be less geometric than those of his predecessors. The hard edges and sharply defined detailing of the earlier modernists became softer, more natural in appearance. Paul remained fascinated by the role of grading in the making of a garden, particularly in the manner of replicating natural form.

Owen Peters came to California from Iowa in 1949. After working for Ralph Smith for six years, he opened his own office and three years later, in 1958, formed a partnership with Bettler Baldwin and Robert Erikkson. Peters had come under the influence of Thomas Church while working in Smith's office, and Erikkson had studied under Eckbo at USC.

Although their practice grew steadily over the years, garden design remained the principal activity of the firm. Peters continued to design gardens, giving every project his personal attention, and like Church and Paul, he always managed to maintain a close relationship with his clients: "We still pride ourselves in doing the highest quality work possible. We try to keep abreast of the changing world, and make every project a contribution to the betterment of society." [76] Like many other landscape architects, Peters' favorite garden is his own.

Donald Brinkerhoff, a homegrown southern Californian, came into landscape architecture through Cal Poly's ornamental horticulture program. Finishing there in 1952, he tried a variety of nursery related jobs before joining the landscape architecture firm of Armstrong and Sharfman in 1956 as a partner. Eric Armstrong had developed a successful Los Angeles practice, and found himself in need of a capable design coordinator, someone to take charge of production of a wide range of projects. Brinkerhoff, largely self-taught in both design and construction, proved more than capable. Like so many garden makers before him, he felt that his education was incomplete, and after practicing on his own for several years, closed his office in 1965 to travel and study abroad—a journey that took him through much of the world over the following three years. In 1968, he returned to California and set about developing a new kind of practice, one which would bring a variety of different views together and would follow the methods and ideas he had been exposed to in his travels. The new firm called Lifescapes was located in Newport Beach, and very quickly became a leading voice in landscape design in southern California.

Top and opposite right: Contemporary southern California estates, with garden design by Donald Brinkerhoff (Lifescapes). The return to Mediterranean and particularly hispanic themes is readily noted.

Above: This tile manufacturer's garden recalls hispanic themes in contemporary usage, by Eriksson, Peters and Thoms. Opposite Left: A view into Owen Peters' garden in Pasadena.

In San Diego, the art of garden design had languished after the departures of Kate Sessions and Paul Thiene, and the invigorating but brief flush of Hispanic development associated with the Panama-California Exposition of 1915. With only limited training in landscape design or horticulture and very little professional ambition, Harriett Wimmer in time filled this void, inheriting as well Kate Sessions' position of preeminence as the city's leading woman gardener. Wimmer was, no doubt, influenced by the great exposition, where as a young woman of seventeen she took pleasure in watching its development in Balboa Park, and later in strolling among its beautifully planted grounds.

She went to Oregon in 1931 to study landscape architecture for a year at the university, returning to San Diego to design gardens occasionally, while pursuing her many charitable and civic interests in the city. Some seventeen years later, following the war and the advent of the modern garden movement in California, Wimmer opened an office of landscape architecture in San Diego, devoted largely to the design of private gardens. But Harriett Wimmer was no modernist. Her gardens reflect a keen awareness of plants and a rather conservative taste for texture, color, variety, and the use of structures in the garden. All of this changed rather

Above: The owner of this Rancho Santa Fe home wanted sculpture in the garden, so landscape architect Joseph Yamada brought James Hubbell, a local sculptor, into the collaborative project to create a striking entry from the street.

the firm's title following her retirement in 1967. Yamada continued to emphasize private garden design in his practice, despite a growing clientele for larger projects:

"The private garden is still the most challenging and satisfying project. The clients' goals are reasonably diverse...furthermore, private gardens force landscape architects to consider the very nature of the garden— sanctuary, retreat, entertainment center, art statement." [77]

Through Yamada, the modern garden thus reached the southern extremities of the state, delineating a design philosophy that connected San Diego to Los Angeles and San Francisco.

abruptly, however, when in 1954 she hired Joseph Yamada, a young graduate of the University of California, Berkeley. Trained altogether in the modern idiom, Yamada quickly expanded what had been largely a carriage-trade practice into a highly successful and widely respected design firm. In 1959, Wimmer asked him to become her full partner.

In respect for her work, as well as for the great friendship that developed between them, Yamada retained her name in

This Page: Contemporary garden above La Jolla combines elements of man-made and natural form with images of sky and sea. Joseph Yamada, landscape architect.

The Decline of Modernism

By the end of the 1960s, garden design seemed to be moving again toward traditionalist Mediterranean revival, not in the style of the 1920s perhaps, but certainly in the preference for earthy colors and adaptations of Hispanic ornamentation and materials. Styles come and go, and come again. If innovative styles like art deco can return to popularity after thirty years or more, so can classic, deep-rooted styles like Mediterranean revival, in all of its forms and by all its titles. Perhaps the Spanish heritage of Old California has proven too enduring and modern form too whimsical or capricious in the eye of the public. The modern garden, however, despite its architectonic nature, its experimentation with the blending of natural and geometric form, and its reductive simplicity in design and materials, is for the most part an original concept, not a stylistic adaptation from the past. This cannot be said of the Mediterranean revivals, either in 1970 or the more creative epoch of the 1920s. How does one recognize original design in the art of garden making or any other art, and separate it from derivative or eclectic borrowing?

Look at two of the better-known gardens of each era. The Donnell garden (1948) may evoke some of the free-flowing expressionism of Le Corbusier or

Picasso—as well as that of surrounding forms of nature itself—yet it remains an original expression of form, purpose, and detail. Its graceful flowing forms unite the composition while at the same time reflecting and underscoring the outlying natural terrain, its angular wood deck extending human domain yet pierced to allow the intrusion of the natural elements. It is at once a modern California garden. On the other hand, the Kirk Johnson garden (1925, see pages 109,112,113), although imaginatively sited in the wooded hills of Montecito, could just as easily have been dropped into the hillsides of sixteenth-century Tuscany. Furthermore, nature was considered to be so much the enemy by Renaissance architects and their clients that the wisdom and logic of geometry was never allowed to yield to whimsical asymmetry, and plants themselves, no matter how beloved, were kept prisoners in pots or captured and paraded in servile form as clipped hedges and pleached or pollarded avenues of greenery.

Originality is the result of a long journey, a generic process that has its beginnings in the social, religious, economic, and political character of the people, as well as in the climate and structure of the land. It comes from a nation's literature and poetry and music, as well as from its stones and wildflowers. And it is in our gardens, more than in our houses, paintings, or even our cities, that we have chosen not only to portray an original expression of modern art, but also the most profound aspect of cultural life in California. The modern garden is not unique to California, nor did it spring fully formed from the drawing boards of California's imaginative and resourceful modern garden makers. But it is here that all the parts—historic derivations, climate, cultural demands—fit together to produce something that is collectively original.

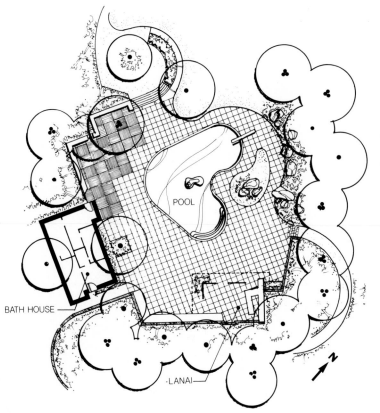

The Dewey Donnell garden, by Thomas Church and Lawrence Halprin, completed in 1948, is now considered a major step in the evolution of the modern California garden. Left: Plan view. Above: a view from under trees that pierce through the deck. At far left, a view across the pool garden into the Sonoma County countryside.

209

The modern garden eventually ran its course. Beginning as a wellspring of imaginative concept and form in the 1930s, it gathered strength and the force of a churning mountain stream in the 1940s, a clear and rapid current in the 1950s, and finally a broad, slow-moving muddy river in the 1960s, eventually meandering and dividing into tributaries of varied value and expressiveness. Four of these can be identified as characteristic garden forms of the 1970s and 1980s.

Mannerist: The modern garden no longer saw involvement in experimentation, either in form or material usage. It was a softening and polishing of modernism, producing, at its best, solid, formula-tested garden design, rendered in time honored materials.

Mediterranean Revival (again!): As modernism in garden design began to lose currency during the 1960s, many landscape architects, no doubt at the behest of clients, returned to the tried-and-true. Instant culture is seen to result from the use of arcaded drives to fountain adorned court-

yards, tiled patios, reflecting pools, adobe-like walls, and axial symmetry.

Post-modernism and its allies: The only garden form of recent times which can be favorably compared to the experimental arts of the 1930s, post-modernism in garden design became the vehicle for readdressing the challenges faced in the early years of modernism, as well as in the continuing expressions of modern art and design through the 1960s. It is also a challenge to landscape architects who abandoned modernism during that decade in favor of other approaches to design. Post-

modernism, which must be viewed as an umbrella for continuing modernist experimentation, usually found its inspiration in artists' studios, galleries and the paintings of minimalist works like latter day modernists Sol Lewitt or Donald Judd. But the most successful proponent of minimalist expression in garden design is Peter Walker of San Francisco, who employs what he calls *seriality*, a kind of rhythmic repetition to achieve order in composition, and *gesture*, or an emphasis on creating visual impact to the garden scheme. In a Walker garden, design is both obvious and contrived—as in a composition by Picasso. Minimalist garden design carries the impulse of Impressionism, while often lacking concern for practical usefulness. The post-modern garden is not a derivative of post-modern architecture, like that of Michael Graves' various projects in California. It was first interpreted by Isamu Noguchi in several California plazas and commercial gardens, and although often considered audacious, it is nonetheless a challenge to garden makers to expand the envelope of artistic possibility.

Ecosystematic: A final tributary, gathering force in the 1990s, is garden design based on ecosystematic criteria. Nearly opposite to the visual criteria of postmodernism, the environmentally aware garden seeks to achieve the maximum in usefulness, with the least expenditure of natural resources. Others who have successfully sought new directions in garden design during the 1980s are Harland Hand in San Francisco, Christine Rosmini in Los Angeles, Campbell and Campbell in Santa Monica, and Isabelle Greene in Santa Barbara. It is the thrust of garden design as the century draws to a close. This is discussed in more detail in the final chapter.

This Page: Detail of patio at the Beckman Center in Irvine, 1988, by Peter Walker and Martha Schwartz (top left).The minimalist approach to courtyard design, by Walker and Schwartz, here at the IBM Center in Santa Teresa (above).

Opposite Page: Richard Garland added this handsome swimming pool to a house in Montecito designed by architect Richard Neutra (top). The return to Mediterranean revival in the 1980s is reflected in this 1990 residence in San Diego, by Gillespie/DeLorenzo, landscape architects (bottom).

The Modern Garden in Summary

The modern movement which exploded on the art world in the 1920s and 1930s was essentially a reaction against the worn, if time-honored, traditions of classicism, in all its forms. Modernism of the arts, so brash and inventive in the beginning became, at last, as worn and time-honored as the styles and methods it had replaced. But like all stylistic trends or design processes, its elements, in some residue or skeletal form, have been retained in varying degrees of eclectic form, as the four tributaries suggest. Certainly this is true for garden design, the heritage of which combines all the elements of California's garden history.

The *rancho* era of Old California and the Mediterranean revival which followed a hundred years later gave the California garden its three basic elements:

Enclosure—adobe walls, an arcade or the walls of the house itself, surrounding, giving finite definition and space, framing and composition.

Connection—a direct relationship of space, function, and form in association with the house, blending them into a single, enlarged living unit. In the old patio garden, the key was to be found in the transition zone, the *corredor*, which included the projecting roofline and supporting posts or columns, and the extension of the interior wood floor to the full width of the *corredor*. Here one was sheltered from the sun but in touch with the breezes and the garden itself.

Centricity—based on custom, the organization of the enclosed space was centric and also centripetal or directed inwards toward a central element—in this case almost always a well or fountain. As life in the arid regions of the world tend to revolve around the source of water, so was it true of the Old California patio.

The modern garden makers in California retained and expanded these basic elements, and added several more:

Enclosure became more complex, with the use of free-standing screens, dividers, walls, and imaginative fencing to separate and direct. These were often made to curve, zig-zag, change shape and material. Enclosure in the modern garden also included directing foot traffic, extending views, as well as creating privacy and dominion.

Connection in the modern garden depended on more than a singular, unchanging transition zone, and often included devices such as the projecting of architectural elements to the extremities of the site, while at the same time drawing garden elements into the house by means of penetrating walls, water features, and panels of glass.

The singular *centric* design concept of Spanish and revival gardens gave way to a more complex formula, consisting of three elements:

Abstraction. In the modern garden, this consists of a simplification or reduction of natural form to basic, elemental shape. Topography would become softly curvilinear, complex mass reduced to a series of planes and angles.

Juxtaposition. For centuries, garden makers had derived form from nature (as in English and Japanese gardens) or from architecture and mathematical principles (as in Italian and French gardens). The modern garden blends the two by abstracting from natural form and applying creative uses to geometry—30, 60, and 45 degree angles, for instance, instead of the usual 90 degrees.

Isabelle Greene in Santa Barbara, 1983.

213

Rhythm. Rhythm, in garden design, as well as in other visual arts, calls for the use of repeating elements, placed in regular or expanding division. A checkerboard paving pattern, a repeating design in a fence detail, the grid in the pattern of brick lay-out, the zig-zag of a retaining or seat wall, the measured spacing of identical plants. Rhythm gives a garden composition a sense of visual movement, but it also adds scale and order to the overall design. While order was rather easily achieved by the singular, centric design of the older eclectic gardens, visual rhythm was necessary in achieving order and organization in the more complex modern garden of the 1930s through the 1960s.

By the late 1970s, however, stylistic concerns in garden design were giving way to other interests, other demands. California was running out of the essential basic ingredients for garden making—land and water. At least in the major metropolitan areas, where population increases continued unabated, the cost of land and the demands for water began to raise a spectre of doubt as to the future of private gardens in the Golden State. During the 1980s, Californians found themselves facing an escalating real estate market which soon priced nearly half of the first-time home buyers out of the single family detached market. New tracts were being built on postage stamp lots as small as 3,500 square feet, and condominiums, the slow-movers of the previous decade, were becoming the primary real estate option for the entry-level homeowner.

At the same time, awareness of damage and misuse of the Earth was becoming more apparent to an increasingly larger percentage of the population in California, as well as the rest of the nation, and along with our concerns about pollution, waste, and the despoilment of nature came a new attitude towards the making of gardens. Space utilization and efficiency of maintenance needed to be addressed, but most importantly we were being asked to take a longer look at what we were planting in our garden. There were those exotics, with special needs for soil amendments, feeding, and water. And there was our imported custom of covering nearly all ground surfaces with ever thirstier green lawns.

In 1933, a Glendora farmer named Orton Englehardt patented his new impact sprinkler head, with an idea towards improving the irrigation of avocado and citrus groves. With his close friends Mary and Clem la Fetra (founders of Rainbird Corporation), the lawn sprinkler concept was developed a year later. But it was not until after the war that lawn sprinklers became readily available to the rapidly expanding tract house market. Lot sizes began to grow accordingly from 5,000 square feet in 1947 to as much as 15,000 square feet in 1965, most of which would by this time be covered in lawn—similar to midwestern tract housing.

Throughout the 1960s and 1970s, Californians chose to cover the outdoors in grass—their private gardens, public parks, school grounds, church yards, industrial complexes, and even their shopping centers. No longer sown by seed or stolon, turfgrass was now being unrolled like a giant green carpet over the parched brown earth—kept alive and healthy by means of Orton Englehardt's lawn sprinklers and a seemingly inexhaustible supply of cheap water. Pop-up and rotary sprinkler heads followed, and garden irrigation systems reminiscent of ancient Andalusia made arid California bloom far beyond the capabilities of the earlier fixed head sprinklers of the 1920s. But by the latter 1980s, the finite nature of land and water had at last become obvious to most people. With the years of drought (1985—1992) serving as a particularly arid reminder, Californians at last began to realize that their future was already upon them.

Opposite: This tile manufacturer's garden recalls hispanic themes in contemporary usage, by Eriksson, Peters and Thoms.

V.

Tomorrow's Garden

The clouds are lifting from the high Sierras,
The Bay mists clearing.
And the angel in the gate, the flowering plum,
Dances like Italy, imagining red.

Louis Simpson

Above: **Sunset** *magazine headquarters in Menlo Park.*

Opposite: Noguchi Gardens, Costa Mesa, California.

People, Land and Water

Every day in California, seven days a week, twelve months a year, the population of the state grows by 1600 new arrivals. Births, snowbirds who come for the winter and decide to stay, business transfers, Mexican, Central American and Asian immigrants seeking a better life, and sundry others in pursuit of hope and adventure—all of these add to the daily population increase. A few disillusioned souls depart the Golden State, usually for the Pacific Northwest's less demanding regimen, or they return to their roots in Iowa and elsewhere—and each day some 750 die. But the net gain for more than thirty years running averages 1600 new Californians every day, the same number, incidentally, as the population of all of Los Angeles in its first census year, 1850.

On that momentous date, the year of statehood, the population for California was estimated to be 93,000—not including Indians. By 1890, the population count passed the one million mark and in 1930 it surpassed five million; ten million in 1950; nearly twenty million in 1970; and by 1990 it had topped thirty million.

Sherman Gardens, Corona Del Mar.

Although California continues to lead the nation in agricultural production and exportation, over 95 percent of the state's population is considered by demographers to be urban. That means that 1520 people each day must find housing in the cities and suburbs—especially the suburbs. This demand accounts for all those housing tracts that are creeping like lava flows through the dry canyons and along the major motorways leading out of San Francisco, Los Angeles, and San Diego. With service costs spiraling upward, state and local officials now find it increasingly difficult to provide for these mushrooming bedroom communities, which stretch from San Francisco to Santa Rosa and east of Los Angeles County past Riverside. The coastal communities north of San Diego, long the summer resort towns of wealthy urbanites, are filling in the beach spaces as well as spilling eastward to swell the populations of dusty agricultural towns like Escondido and Fallbrook and planned communities like Rancho California and Rancho Santa Fe, with names intended to provide them with instant heritage.

Despite the economic downturn of the early 1990s, most forecasters continued to predict an ever-broadening population spiral. Where, some wondered, would the land and the resources be found to accommodate growth? The developers and real estate speculators who thrive in this vortex simply point to a supply of seemingly endless vistas of scrubby terrain in the inland valleys, where little in the way of farming or grazing now exists. There is no shortage of land for development, they insist. The Indians and rancheros of pre-state times might have managed to survive in the Antelope Valley or on the bleak, sand-swept stretches along the eastern slope of the Sierras, or across the San Luis River valley where the Pala Indian Reservation still survives to this day, doing things in the old ways. But modern man requires a newspaper and a lifeline of services—energy, transportation, amusement, provisions, and most of all, water. Water conservation is a constant concern throughout the state, as it has been since the days of the *dons*, but during a prolonged drought that began in the late 1980s, concern eventually reached critical levels requiring government intervention in the early 1990s.

Opposite top: A front lawn becomes a water-conscious garden in southern California.

Opposite bottom: Crescent Bay Park, Laguna Beach, is a pleasant open space in an otherwise crowded and exclusive area of ocean front properties. Gillespie/DeLorenzo, landscape architects.

Water Needs

Southern California, with the least amount of locally available water and the greatest potential population growth rate, had anticipated its future water needs at the turn of the century and had acted decisively—or as some have said, treacherously—in its own interest. In a move that could have been lifted directly from a movie script of the old west, William Mulholland, Los Angeles' chief engineer, concocted a monumental plan that could produce a constant flow of water into the metropolitan area, sufficient for the foreseeable future and beyond. It was 1913, and Los Angeles, with frontier-like bravado, obtained water rights to the adjacent San Fernando Valley and then moved north, acquiring most of the Owens Valley, which constituted the watershed for the rivers draining the southern Sierra Nevada range. Then began the construction of a two-hundred mile aqueduct to carry this captive water to a thirsty town. Within two years, the citrus industry surrounding Los Angeles doubled and then re-doubled in both quantity and production.

It was still not enough to satisfy the needs for a rapidly expanding city. In 1928, with the formation of the Metropolitan Water District (MWD—made up of Los Angeles and twelve other thirsty local towns), the water-gatherers looked eastward, towards the mighty Colorado River, nemesis of early explorers, border between California and Arizona, and principal drainage system of the entire Southwest. Here on the muddy banks of the great river, engineers laid the ground-

work for a second aqueduct to serve Los Angeles. With considerable assistance from the federal government, which built both Parker and Hoover dams, the Colorado River Aqueduct was completed in 1941, running a distance of 242 miles from river to metropolis.

Not to be outdone, San Francisco also anticipated the need for imported water early in the twentieth century. This fact was made obvious to the city when in 1906 the devastating earthquake struck and the subsequent fires destroyed most of downtown's wooden structures, there being no adequate water supply for such unforeseen calamities.

But just 170 miles to the east of the city lay the Hetch Hetchy Valley, nearly as beautiful as the revered Yosemite, a few miles to the south. Here, on the watershed of the Tuolumne River and its tributaries, San Francisco's mayor James Phelan unveiled his grand plan to insure the city's future growth, if not its salvation. But damming the scenic valley in order to achieve a constant water supply for the distant city attracted the attention of early environmentalists, particularly the Sierra Club's John Muir, preservationist and champion of California's newly established national parks (Sequoia and Yosemite in 1890). For more than eight years of wearying litigation, Muir held up construction of the complex aqueduct system (which would have to be tunneled through twenty-five miles of the Coastal Range). Eventually, however, Phelan and the city prevailed, and the controversial project was at last completed in 1928. The difficulty and cost, however, of negotiating the rugged terrain, together with the persistent opposition to additional water-carrying projects, have resulted in the city's reliance to a great extent on local wells for much of its domestic water supply.

Local wells, fed by underground aquifers and mountain stream run-off, proved to be a cheaper, if less dependable, source of water for many north coast towns. In the south, Santa Barbara also came to depend on local wells and run-off from the Sierra Madre range into Lake Cachuma. Having been given the chance to join Los Angeles' Metropolitan Water District in its early going, Santa Barbara declined, dreading an expected population growth more than the possible consequences of drought. As a result of this decision, Santa Barbara became the first California city to impose severe water rationing in recent times (1989), including a ban on garden watering altogether in 1990. The elaborate Mediterranean revival gardens of the 1920s, having long been served themselves by on-site wells, suffered less than the average residential gardens in the city.

Other California cities began to initiate water-conserving ordinances during the drought years, as water levels in lakes and reservoirs throughout the state fell to dangerously low levels. Novato, near San Francisco, offered to pay homeowners fifty dollars for every one hundred square feet of lawn that was replaced by water-conserving plantings.

Opposite: Wall detail to catch the afternoon shadows, Santa Barbara.

San Francisco mandated a 25 percent reduction in domestic water usage and imposed a stiff surcharge for going over limit. Tiny Orange Cove in the central valley, a town with no water meters for domestic usage, asked its citizens to restrict their water usage to ten gallons a person per day—two flushes.

Los Angeles, with its powerful Metropolitan Water District, has fared better than even the wettest parts of the state. After completion in 1971 of the controversial State Water Project, which captured water from several northern rivers and channeled it southward, the city and its many subsidiary users appeared to be safe from serious water shortages for the foreseeable future—as Mulholland had long before promised. But by 1991 Los Angeles, like most California cities, was facing emergency rationing, carrying a 30-50 percent cut-back for all MWD user clients. Although the drought conditions of five years lessened somewhat during the winter rains of 1991-92, most experts believed that California would continue to face a future of insufficient water, dry wells, and half-empty reservoirs. To their credit, the commissioners of MWD voted to alter their original charter in order to include environmental protection among the principal goals in future planning, further delaying the construction of costly new water-carrying systems like the proposed Peripheral Canal. The message from MWD to its clients in 1992 clearly read: less water, higher cost.

Opposite: The Indian Wells model home uses soft desert tones to reduce glare and complement the stucco color of the residence. Landscape architects., Peridian.

Water Conserving Gardens

What effect has all of this had in recent years on the profession of landscape architecture, particularly on garden making in California? Indeed, what might all this emphasis on conservation, coupled with rising real estate costs, mean for the future of the California garden itself? Considering the problems of water shortages, shrinking lot sizes, and spiraling construction costs that are pricing the average homeowner out of the single-family detached housing market, one wonders: will there even be a California garden in our future?

Some significant steps have been taken lately, in both technology and design, to address these concerns. In both northern and southern California, for example, Xeriscape Conferences have been established since the mid-1980s to provide data on water conservation to landscape architects, the landscape industry, and interested members of the general public. Such things as water-conserving irrigation equipment, drought-tolerant plant material, and water-conscious garden design are featured at these yearly expositions. The Xeriscape Conference is an opportunity for landscape professionals to learn about new products, as well as design principles for reducing water needs from residential to agricultural usage. In this way, industry professionals have been introduced to drip irrigation, nearly fric-

tionless poly-vinylchloride pipe, low-pressure sprinkler heads, (and spring loaded pop-ups), bubblers, backflow prevention valves, shutoff valves (developed by Toro), which prevent loss of water from damaged heads, and other advances in the plumbing industry, along with water-absorbing polymer soil additives for the purpose of increasing the efficiency of water delivery.

Above: A hispanic styled shopping center in La Verne turns its back to Foothill Boulevard traffic (destroyed in 1991).

Opposite: The Ritz Carlton Rancho Mirage. Landscape architects, Peridian.

Through the efforts of Xeriscape, many California plant nurseries, both retail and wholesale, have made native and other drought-tolerant plants more readily available. In addition, water saving methods of grading and drainage have been imposed in cities like Davis to reduce storm run-off loss and improve local water storage and percolation systems on individual lots.

In addition to the state's various techniques for acquiring and storing what must be our most important renewable resource, expanded methods for reuse of water are helping California to reduce growing shortages. Water treatment plants, now located throughout California's urban areas, are equipped with pumping plants which return treated water to rivers and aquifers and replenish water tables and ground water levels. The new San Jose Treatment Plant, with pumping station on the San Gabriel River east of Los Angeles, is an example. Recycled water from treatment plants and desalinization of ocean water represent future sources of water for the state's ever-increasing demands.

In respect to water-conscious design, landscape architects began to use more hard surfaces in place of grass: unglazed tile, brick, exposed aggregate, stamped concrete, wood decking, and less expensive materials such as river gravel, decomposed granite, wood chips, and even raked earth to reduce water consumption.

In the lower inland valleys, away from the mitigating effect of gentle marine air currents, intense summer heat remains a major concern in garden design, equal to that of water conservation. During an unusually hot spell in June of 1990, one Claremont gardener was amazed to see how well her newly planted snow-in-summer and rockrose had stood up to 110 degrees Fahrenheit, while her English ivy withered and burned despite the drenching it had received. Surely, green lawns and lush plantings may soften the impact of intense summer heat, if only in an illusionary way, but the ancient methods of sun control, employed from the times of the Moorish gardens, provide more realistic answers to exposure. If the garden of the future is to be composed largely of paved and graveled surfaces, planters, drought-resistant shrubs and ground covers, it will also require shade giving plants and structures—trees, arbors, vine-covered trellises, awnings, and lath. Raised planters can be used to create needed breaks in paved surfaces, and at a height of only twelve inches, can effectively screen off eight or ten feet of pavement from a seated person. Of course, any use of plant material—a tracery of vines, a shade tree casting a leafy, fluttering shadow, edging plants or a few well-placed tubs, or even rows of clay pots filled with colorful annuals can effectively soften paved surfaces.

In the era of the depression, when money for garden making was in greater scarcity than water, Thomas Church led the way in creating efficient and useful gardens requiring little maintenance and water. Since our lawns can account for nearly 90 percent of both water usage

and energy expenditure in the garden, the ethics of early Californians, as well as modernist designers like Church, must be adapted to future garden planning.

Gardening practices, whether derived from the restraints imposed by the Great Depression or the limited technology of the Franciscan padres, ought to employ practical principles of conservation. Technology itself has often held out false promises: cheap water and cheap electrical power, creating artificial oases and unnatural climates. But restricted resources now require us to live in closer harmony with the natural world, and to accept its rhythms.

Our principal legacy in respect to a garden ethic is inherited from the mission and rancho gardeners and reinforced in both the Mediterranean revival and modern garden eras. Not only have they given us a proper foundation in the technology of water conservation, but also and more importantly, they have provided us with an enduring attachment to gardens and garden design. This garden ethic, which was largely developed in the private sector, has spread to most aspects of public outdoor living in California, and despite ongoing and future water restrictions, promises to remain a major characteristic of what we call the California lifestyle.

Below: 1915 Expo buildings continue to serve San Diego's Balboa Park, as seen here in the local artists' courtyard. Opposite: Weather worn bench maintains its charm and place in the California garden.

Heritage
of the
California
Garden

Most contemporary malls, especially
those of the 1990s Mediterranean revival,
include some garden-like sitting areas for
weary shoppers, and a nearby *restaurant*
is nearly certain to have an attached outdoor dining area—a patio garden shaded
by a trellis of wisteria or trumpet vine.
And the floor will be unglazed Mexican
tile or flagstone, brick or a combination of
several materials. Patrons in the garden
restaurant will relax over their coffee in an
atmosphere enhanced by purplish bougainvillea and murmurs of a bubbling fountain, separated from the crush of passing
shoppers by cleverly placed planters,
wrought-iron scrollwork, and glazed tile
surfaces. Regardless of the style, such
restaurants have one thing in common—
the best qualities of a garden.

Opposite: Californians are at home outdoors, in
their own gardens as well as in garden restaurants
like Lawry's California Center in Los Angeles.

Garden restaurants, whether or not attached to malls and shopping centers, have been a California institution for many years. Following the rebuilding of Santa Barbara after the 1925 earthquake, the prevailing Mediterranean architectural theme included garden restaurants like the Presidio Cafe overlooking fashionable State Street. In keeping with the Spanish theme of the second exposition in San Diego's Balboa Park, the Cafe del Rey Moro, set in an exotic subtropical garden, remains a favorite Sunday brunch stop for locals and visitors. Recently developed shopping centers like The Mercado Village in San Juan Capistrano and The Del Mar Plaza in Del Mar, by Emmet Wemple, are well served by attractive garden restaurants—in more contemporary Mediterranean motif. In truth, wherever one travels in California, from San Diego to San Francisco, at any rate, a garden restaurant awaits the weary tourist and shopper alike.

Top: Bazaar Del Mundo, 'Old Town' San Diego.

Middle: For many years a popular brunch stop in Balboa Park, the Cafe del Rey Moro is a San Diego institution for outdoor eating.

Left: The Del Mar Plaza, 1990, ingeniously planned to maximize foot traffic, ocean views; direct access from surface streets, hidden parking below. Good garden restaurants are among its major attraction. Emmet Wemple, landscape architect.

Opposite Page: The Four Seasons Hotel in Beverly Hills, completed in 1987, has several garden areas for relaxing, gathering and dining. Don Brinkerhoff, landscape architect, Lifescapes (top). Bandini's restaurant patio 'Old Town', San Diego (bottom).

Our garden legacy is found in public institutions as well. The city library in San Juan Capistrano was designed by Michael Graves, and in the full blush of post-modernism of the late 1980s, created a heated debate among art patrons and the local populace. More important than its stylistic values or drawbacks, however, are the many gardens and courtyards neatly interspersed within the wings of the building itself. Large windows lead the eye of the most dedicated researcher into the garden, where hummingbirds are at work on the climbing honeysuckle. One may even find a niche for study in the garden itself, without actually leaving the confines of the library.

The garden has also become a necessary element in many California workplaces, from small office to giant industrial complex. In the late 1950s, the Stuart pharmaceutical plant in Pasadena, by architect Edward Stone and Thomas Church and Lawrence Halprin, was one

of the first to recognize the need to provide a pleasant environment for employees during non-working hours. Today, many industrial plants provide active recreation programs, as well as relaxing garden areas in order to combat stress-related duties and to create a homelike atmosphere at work. Royston, Hanamoto, Alley and Abey, being landscape architects who practice what they preach, have developed a pleasant garden for their employees in Mill Valley, which includes a patio under old redwoods and ancient California bay trees overlooking a natural stream.

This Page: San Juan Capistrano Library—fountain detail. Designed by Michael Graves (below). Noguchi Gardens, Costa Mesa. Designed by Isamu Noguchi (left).

Opposite Page: Alexander Haagen office building, Landscape architects, Peridian (top). Pasadena Civic Center (bottom).

California's mild climate is no doubt responsible, in part, for the growing number of *sculpture gardens* in the Golden State. Some of these are attached to major museums, like the Los Angeles County Museum of Art and Balboa Park's Museum of Fine Arts in San Diego. The sculpture garden is also well represented on university campuses, such as the Franklin D. Murphy Sculpture Garden at UCLA, the Hillside Garden at the Art Center College, Pasadena, and the more informal sculpture garden at Long Beach State. The sculpture garden at the Norton Simon Museum in Pasadena is particularly well received, as are the gardens at the J. Paul Getty Museum in Malibu, which were designed by Wemple. Sculp-

ture seems enhanced by a garden setting, and many artists plan their work to consider changing patterns of light and shadow, the textural contrasts afforded by various plantings.

The *garden theatre* is making something of a comeback in California, especially on college campuses. Pomona College in Claremont makes use of an amphitheatre built in the 1920s, while nearby Scripps College stages small productions in its Moorish styled Margaret Fowler Garden. In Topanga, Shakespeare and other dramatists reign at the Theatricum Botanicum, a garden theatre founded by actor Will Geer and his friends. Many California cities maintain open-air amphitheatres, like The

Redlands Bowl, for summer evenings devoted to the music of Rudolph Friml or Gilbert and Sullivan. The largest and longest running outdoor production in California however is *Ramona*, performed by a cast of hundreds (if not thousands) each year at the Ramona Bowl near Hemet.

This Page: Sculpture garden by Robert Carter, landscape architect, c. 1965.

Opposite Page: California's museums and libraries have always boasted patios and enclosed garden spaces. Clockwise from top: The J. Paul Getty Museum garden in Malibu by Emmet Wemple, the Museum of Contemporary Art in Los Angeles, and the 1930s Clark Library garden by Ralph Cornell in Los Angeles.

The *community garden*, although usually associated with growing food, has developed into a sociable recreational institution in many Los Angeles neighborhoods, just as the semiprivate gardens of condominium developments have aided in strengthening social bonds through a common need and use not easily attained in single family housing tracts. Although condominium living is relatively new to many Californians, such developments as Baldwin Hills Village (The Village Green) have long demonstrated that community gardens, whether designed for recreation, relaxation or food production, can stabilize and augment neighborhood well being. Under the auspices of a community garden association, many a vacant lot in south-central Los Angeles has been converted into a productive garden venture, providing food, social activity, and community pride to the surrounding residential blocks.

California is also rich in *botanic gardens*, many with special collections or specific research programs. (A few of the better known of these are listed at the conclusion of this chapter). Many botanic gardens, including the Los Angeles

County Arboretum in Arcadia; the Descanso Gardens in La Canada; the Strybling Garden in Golden Gate Park, San Francisco; Rancho Santa Ana Botanic Garden in Claremont; Quail Gardens in Encinitas; and Filoli in Woodside also sell plants to the public and most of them include demonstration gardens to illustrate home use of readily available water conserving plants.

Below: Balboa Park, San Diego.

Left: The Fragrance Garden for the blind at Strybling Garden, within Golden Gate Park. Landscape architect was Edward Williams, EDAW.

Opposite: Baldwin Hills (now the Village Green), a 1939-40 experiment in cluster housing, superblock, and shared open space, by Robert Alexander and Reginald Johnson, with landscape architect Fred Barlow Jr., Los Angeles.

Opposite Bottom: The Lakes, Irvine condominum project, landscape architect, Lifescapes.

College and university campuses throughout the state have gardens of widely ranging styles and uses, from the cloister-like patios of Scripps College (by Edward Huntsman-Trout), to the experimental food-and-flower garden at the University of California, Santa Cruz. The California Institute of Technology boasts the famous Athenaeum courtyard (by Florence Yoch) which serves as a garden reception room, outdoor dining room, and formal gathering area. California State Polytechnic University in Pomona maintains the renowned Kellogg Rose Garden, which was established by Charles Gibbs Adams before the famous Arabian horse ranch became a university.

Public gardens, reminiscent of Europe's nineteenth-century romantic parks, with their picturesque lagoons and fusty formality, are becoming popular again, as exemplified by Santa Barbara's Alice Keck Memorial Garden. Here are found the singular strollers, the mothers with toddlers and baby

buggies, the lovers holding hands, the reader on the bench, the girl feeding the ducks. No joggers, par-course activists, frisbee chasing dogs or basketball backstops are likely to be seen here. When the private garden is not an option, such passive places become urban havens from the pressures of the world. Birds and butterflies welcome the visitor, and such idyllic gardens can be expected to play a greater role in the future, as Californians in increasing numbers begin to occupy the townhouses, apartments, and condominiums that are closer to the inner city and to their workplaces.

In 1958 William Penn Mott, Jr. warned San Franciscans of the need to protect existing open space and acquire more green area for the city's densely populated urban areas:

"No other area in the United States is more favored than this San Francisco Bay region, but we have probably done less with our natural resources than other similar areas. The next twenty-five years should be devoted to the preservation of large areas surrounding our Bay....New materials and construction techniques, together with an abundance of plant material, make it possible to develop beautiful and colorful parks beyond the scope normally available in other areas." [78]

Above: A path through a section of Rancho Santa Ana Botanic Garden, Claremont.

*Opposite: **Romeo and Juliet** are performed on campus by students of Pitzer College, Claremont.*

Opposite Top: The Margaret Fowler Memorial Garden at Scripps College, Claremont, designed by Edward Huntsman-Trout, is used by theatre students for occasional summer productions.

Changes have occurred certainly. Mott, a California landscape architect, went from superintendent of Oakland's parks to director of the National Park Service during that twenty-five years, but his pleas for public garden space in San Francisco remain largely unanswered:

"In addition, throughout the concentrated portions of the Bay Area we should be planning small parks, plazas and triangles, not only for their beauty and open space, but to add points of interest and color to our sometimes drab city developments. Unless we are willing to change our thinking from the horse and buggy era and advance with the atomic future, park and recreation people may lose a great opportunity to make our urban communities attractive, beautiful places in which to live, and to make living in urban centers pleasant and satisfying through productive, imaginative programs for the people's increasing leisure time." [79]

Have we changed our thinking regarding open space in urban centers for San Francisco or Fresno, or any other California city? During those twenty-five years and more that have passed since Mott's warning, have we lost "the great opportunity" that he advocated?

Opposite: Sherman Gardens in Corona del Mar.

Bottom Right: Site line of central courtyard, Ambassador College, Pasadena. Landscape architect was Garrett Eckbo for EDAW.

Bottom Left: Rancho Santa Ana Botanical Garden, originally located in Santa Ana and moved to Claremont in the early 1950s, maintains one of the most complete collections of California native plants and cultivars. Here pictured in May are California poppies, wild iris, and meadow foam.

Middle: The Kallam Memorial Perennial Garden, Los Angeles State and County Arboretum, is a newly developed demonstration garden promoting use of water-conscious perennials. Shirley Kerins, landscape architect.

Top and opposite: The Transamerica garden in downtown San Francisco, with its enclosing forest of coast redwoods, has become a popular retreat from noise and congestion in the inner city. Guzzardo and Associates, landscape architects.

Above: The courtyard of the Pasadena Police Department was the result of an arts commission competition for the purpose of displaying local artwork, won by Campbell and Campbell, landscape architects.

Now as the next millennium approaches, there are signs that we are beginning to realize that efficiency in all things must replace expedience and unchallenged production.

During the early years of economic growth in the state, we dealt with mushrooming population increases by simply raising the levels of production. This attitude brought us to where we find ourselves today—facing rapidly decreasing resources, as well as the degradation of natural beauty and the loss of wilderness and wildlife. With the state's continuing rapid rate of population expansion, efficiency in the use of our remaining resources, rather than expediency in utilizing such resources that still remain, seems all the more obvious. When the demand for water outreaches the supply, for example, what water uses will cease to exist? A future drought coupled with the water demands of 40 million people in the year 2000 would prove disastrous if long-range water conservation plans are not developed.

Could gardens survive in such an undisciplined future, or will California come to resemble the Spain of the Visagoths—an arid, desiccated landscape where clay shards and stone fragments recall reservoirs, aqueducts, and the gardens of a once-productive culture? Can we save the California garden from such a future? Of course we must. No matter how small, simple in design, or limited in plant varieties, it will remain our private place.

Outdoor living, rooted in Spanish tradition and an agreeable climate, remains the enduring truth of the California garden. The various examples of this garden heritage described above underscore this truth, and further demonstrate a garden's importance in the life of a Californian.

In the future, more of us will doubtless come to depend upon public gardens for outdoor living. Interests, needs and design style will change as well, but the garden—in concept—will remain. Nothing about California is more constant, more natural, more necessary. Our gardens sustain us in today's pressing, competitive society. Our enclosed garden patio, our garden seat, our place in the sun, this is truly our California legacy.

*　*　*

Today is the first day of spring. The rain has been falling off and on now for five days and masses of gray cloud contrast with the puffs of cumulus that streak across patches of open blue sky—warning of the onset of yet another advancing storm system. The mountain tops, revealed now and again, glisten white, and the wind comes in sudden gusts, sending showers of tiny green elm flowers through the air.

In the front garden, where last December the turf was replaced with water-conserving rosemary, verbena, thyme, garlic, snow-in-summer, euryops, bearded iris, day lily, and miniature roses, a rainbow of color is bursting forth—crimson, gold, pink, cobalt, lavender, snowy white. And in the shaded patio adjoining the studio, the sun pokes through the speeding clouds in sudden flashes of light, projecting shadowed bamboo canes across the weathered red tiles. A hummingbird hovers over the nandina for an instant and is gone.

Opposite: Balboa Park, San Diego.

246

Noteworthy California Gardens
That Are Open To The Public

Northern California

Strybling Arboretum (Golden Gate Park), San Francisco
　　　9th Avenue and Lincoln Way
　　　Demonstration gardens, trees of the world.

Luther Burbank Memorial Gardens, Santa Rosa
　　　Santa Rosa and Sonoma Avenues
　　　Collection emphasizes Burbank's introductions.

Lane Publishing Company, Menlo Park
　　　Willow and Middlefield Roads
　　　Collection features native plants, design by
　　　Thomas Church.

Villa Montalvo Arboretum, Saratoga
　　　15400 Montalvo Road
　　　Formal garden with emphasis on natives.

Filoli, Woodside (by reservation)
　　　Cañada Road off I-280
　　　Formal estate (1916-17) by Bruce Porter
　　　Excellent example of Mediterranean Revival
　　　garden.

Southern California

Los Angeles State and County Arboretum, Arcadia
　　　301 North Baldwin Avenue
　　　Excellent overall collection, special water
　　　conservation gardens.
　　　Homeowner demonstration gardens.
　　　Historic buildings, Hugo Reid Adobe.

Rancho Santa Ana Botanic Garden, Claremont
　　　1500 North College Avenue
　　　Exclusively native California plants.
　　　Demonstration gardens.
　　　Excellent display gardens, revamped in 1991.

Quail Botanic Gardens, Encinitas
　　　230 Quail Garden Drive
　　　California natives plus subtropical collection
　　　of note.

Descanso Gardens, La Cañada-Flintridge
　　　1418 Descanso Drive
　　　Excellent, well maintained gardens.
　　　Roses and annual color gardens.

Huntington Gardens, San Marino
　　　1151 Oxford Road
　　　Exotics, esp. desert plants of the world, palms,
　　　Australian collection, Shakespeare garden.

Lotusland, Montecito (by reservation)
　　　695 Ashley (at Sycamore Canyon Road)
　　　Well maintained collections, arranged by color
　　　as well as family House and original garden
　　　date from 1926

South Coast Botanic Garden, Palos Verdes
　　　26300 Crenshaw Boulevard
　　　California natives, especially annuals
　　　and wildflowers.

Santa Barbara Botanic Garden, Santa Barbara
　　　1212 Mission Canyon Road
　　　Mostly California natives in a natural setting.
　　　Good collection of Channel Island plants.

Hearst's Castle, San Simeon
　　　State Highway One, near Cambria
　　　Gardens play second fiddle to monumental
　　　eclectic architecture.

Sherman Gardens
　　　2647 East Coast Highway
　　　Corona Del Mar
　　　Traditionally displayed gardens in elegant settings
　　　on a smaller scale.

Notes

1. *"Deep Purple"*, by Mitchell Parish and Peter D. Rose was a popular favorite in 1939.

2. In *Anza Conquers The Desert*, Richard Pourade describes the great overland adventure, using the diary of Franciscan missionary fray, Pedro Font, who was assigned to the journey because of his knowledge of geography and mathematics. Born in Catalonia, Spain he was working at the Mission San Jose de Los Pimas in Sonora when elected to be scribe to Anza. P. 173.

3. Ibid. Font was no botanist and his descriptions of plant material are not precise, if nonetheless enthusiastic. P. 179.

4. Ibid. The precise location for this description of San Francisco Bay is not known, but it was certainly near or on the site of the future presidio. P. 191.

5. Ibid, P. 191.

6. Sanchez, Nellie; *Spanish Arcadia*, P. 273

7. Ibid, P. 91.

8. Garner, William Robert; *Letters From California*, P. 139

9. Ibid, P. 139.

10. Dana, Richard Henry; *Two Years Before the Mast*, P. 77. Dana's sea voyage to California aboard both the Alert and the Pilgrim in the years 1835-6 give us one of our best contemporary accounts of life in Mexican Santa Barbara, San Diego and Monterey.

10a. McDougal, Jane, journal ed. from *Ho For California!*, p.10-11. Mrs. McDougal accompanied her husband John to California in 1848, by way of Panama, along with hordes of gold seekers. John McDougal later became the state's second governor.

11. Ford, Tirey; *Dawn Of The Dons*, P. 130.

12. Ibid, P. 132.

13. Padilla, Victoria; *Southern California Gardens*, P. 31 Padilla, while a professor of English at Los Angeles City College, took a great deal of interest in the early California gardens and the pioneers in horticulture acquainted with Theodore Payne, Roland Hoyt, Hugh Evans, Mildred Mathias, William Hertrich and many other horticulturists and garden designers of the early 20th century. Her book, published in 1961, was the first attempt at a California garden history.

14. Garner, Bess Adams; *Windows in An Old Adobe*, P. 31-34. This book describes in detail the life of the Palomares family at Rancho San Jose in Pomona.

15. DeNevi, Don; *Sketches Of Early California*, P. 17. This book is a collection of contemporary writings concerning life in Pastoral California. The quote is taken from an account by Guadalupe Vallejo, nephew to Mexico's commanding general in northern California, Mariano Vallejo—for whom the Bay Area city is named.

16. Garner, William Robert; *Letters From California*, P. 135.

17. DeNevi, Don; *Sketches of Early California*, P. 18.

18. Fox, Helen Morganthau; *Patio Gardens*, P. 3. Fox was one of the Grand Tour visitors to Europe, who came home full of enthusiasm for Spanish gardens and their application to southern California.

19. Byne, Mildred and Arthur; *Spanish Gardens and Patios*, P. 9.

20. Burton, Richard; *The Perfumed Garden*, P. 82. The original 15th century manuscript was discovered by British occupational forces in the middle of the 19th century. Burton, the adventurer, scholar and all around soldier of fortune, translated this ancient sex manual into English.

21. Dubos, Rene; *Celebrations Of Life*, P. 54. Dubos philosophizes over the different value systems between French and American people, using garden design—in at least this one instance—as a measuring device.

22. Newcomb, Rexford; *The Old Mission Churches and Historic Houses of California*, P. 355. Newcomb, an east coast architect, visited California in 1920s to study the mission and adobe ruins, often finding them superior in design to the eclectic architecture that was being produced in his time.

23. *"The Desert Song,"* written by Sigmund Romberg in 1926. It was a romantic operetta which took advantage of the current appeal of "The Shiek" and the personal cult of Rudolph Valentino.

24. Dobyns, Winifred; *California Gardens*, P. 17. This book remains the principal source for garden taste in California during the 1920s.

25. Ibid, P. 20.

26. *"Stardust,"* written by Hoagy Carmichael in 1927. In 1929 Mitchell Parish added the haunting, romantic words.

27. Thiene, Paul; *"An Old World Garden in a New World Setting,"* American Landscape Architect, August, 1929. P. 14.

Notes

28. Hanson, Archibald E.; *An Arcadian Landscape: The California Gardens of A.E. Hanson, (1920-1932)*, P. 10. The author's memoir, with a descriptive introduction by David Gebhard.

29. Ibid, P.7.

30. Hanson, Archibald E.; Letter to the author, November, 1979. Until his death, Hanson remained in touch with his profession and his gardens. His drawings are archived at UC Santa Barbara.

31. Hanson, Archibald E.; *An Arcadian Landscape,* P. 11.

32. Wharton, Edith; *Italian Villas And Their Gardens*, P. 11. Wharton, better known for her Gothic novels, is the aunt of landscape architect Beatrix Jones, a founding member of The American Society of Landscape Architects in 1899, who she married Max Farrand, Director of The Huntington Library in San Marino, California.

33. Gross, Susan; *"The Gardens of Edward Huntsman-Trout"* (unpublished thesis), Dept. of Landscape Architecture, California State Polytechnic University, 1976. P. 21.

34. Ibid, P. 21.

35. Ibid, P. 18.

36. Ibid, P. 19.

37. Alexander, Robert; article on The Village Green, *Los Angeles Times*, May 29, 1990.

38. *"Do Re Mi,"* Written by Woody Guthrie; recorded by RCA April 26, 1940.

39. Church, Thomas Dolliver; *Gardens Are For People*, P. 97.

40. Ibid, P. 4.

41. Ibid, P. 12.

42. Ibid, P. 148-51.

43. Ibid, P. 53.

44. Ibid, P. 2.

45. Ibid, P. 30.

46. Ibid, P. 35.

47. Morley, G.L. McCann; Forward to *"Contemporary Landscape Architecture,"* Exhibit folio from the San Francisco Museum of Art, February 12, 1937. P. 13.

48. Hitchcock, Henry-Russell, Jr.; *"Contemporary Land scape Architecture,"* P. 15.

49. Eckbo, Garrett; *Landscape For Living*, P. 10.

50. Ibid, P. 15.

51. Ibid, P. 19.

52. Ibid, P. 36.

53. Steele, Fletcher; *"Modern Architecture"*, Contemporary Landscape Architecture, P. 23-25.

54. Eckbo, Garrett; *"The Esthetic of Planting"*, Landscape Design, P. 17-18.

55. Church, Thomas; *"Transition, 1937-1948"*, Landscape Design, ibid. P. 14-15.

56. Eckbo, Garrett; *Urban Landscape Design*, ibid. P. 3.

57. Malnic, Eric, *"Azusa,"* Los Angeles Times, June 12, 1990.

58. Keats, John; *The Crack In The Picture Window*, P. 7.

59. Reynolds, Malvina; *"Little Boxes,"* Cassandra Records, Berkeley, California. Reynolds is one of the original writers of protest songs of the 1960s.

60. Tunnard, C. and Caneel-Claes, J.; *"Manifesto,"* 1937.

61. Tunnard, C.; Statement for *"The Swedish Garden Architects' Association,"* Paris, 1937.

62. Tunnard, C.; *Gardens In The Modern Landscape,* P. 80.

63. Halprin, Lawrence; Interview with author, December 15, 1990.

64. Ibid.

65. Ibid

66. Pepper, Stephen C.; *"Introduction To Garden Design,"* Landscape Design, P. 5.

67. Ibid, P. 5.

68. Dean, Francis; Letter to the author, January 10, 1991.

69. Royston, Robert; Letter to Ervin Zube, 1990.

70. Halprin, Lawrence; Interview with Author, December 15, 1990.

71. Eckbo, G.; *Urban Landscape Design*, P. 3.

72. Wemple, Emmet; Letter to author, December 5, 1990.

73. Ibid.

74. Paul, Courtland; Interview with author, March 27, 1991.

75. Ibid.

76. Peters, Owen; Letter to author, April 2, 1991.

77. Yamada, Joseph; Letter to the author, April 9, 1991.

78. Mott, William Penn, Jr.; *"Parks and Recreation"*, Landscape Architecture, P. 21.

79. Ibid.

Photo Credits

Bibliography

Brookes, John; *Gardens of Paradise*, Weidenfeld and Nicolson, London, 1987.

Burton, Richard; *The Book Of A Thousand Nights And A Night*, Kama Shastra Society, London, 1885.

Burton, Richard (translated by); *The Perfumed Garden of Sheik Nefzawi*, G.F. Putnam, New York, 1964.

Byne, Mildred and Arthur, *Spanish Gardens And Patios*, J.B. Lippincott and Co., Philadelphia and London, 1924.

Church, Thomas, *Gardens Are For People*, Reinhold Company, New York, 1955.

Church, Thomas, *"Transition: 1937-1948,"* Landscape Design, San Francisco Museum of Art, San Francisco, 1948.

Crump, Spencer, *California's Spanish Missions*, Trans-Anglo Books, Corona Del Mar, CA , 1975.

Dana, Richard Henry; *Two Years Before The Mast*, Airmont Books, New York, 1965 (originally published in Boston, 1840).

Davis, William Heath; *Seventy-five Years In California*: Recollections and remarks by one who visited those shores in 1831, and again in 1833, and except when absent on business was a resident from 1838 until the end of a long life, in 1909, J. Howell Books (3rd ed.), San Francisco, 1967.

DeNevi, Don; *Sketches Of Early California: A Collection Of Personal Adventures*, Chronicle Books, San Francisco, 1971.

Dobyns, Winifred Starr; *California Gardens*, MacMillan and Company, New York, 1931.

Donley, Michael et al, *Atlas Of California*, Pacific Book Center, Culver City, CA, 1979.

Dubos, Rene, *Celebrations Of Life*, McGraw-Hill Company, New York, 1981.

Eckbo, Garrett; *Landscape For Living*, F.W. Dodge Company, New York, 1950.

Eckbo, Garrett; *Home Landscape (The Art Of Home Landscaping)*, McGraw-Hill Company, New York, 1956.

Eckbo, Garrett, *Urban Landscape Design,* McGraw-Hill Company, New York, 1964.

Eckbo, Garrett, *"The Esthetics of Planting,"* Landscape Design, San Francisco Museum of Art, San Francisco, 1948.

Fay, James et al; *California Almanac, 1985*, Presidio Press, Novato, CA, 1985.

Ford, Tirey; *Dawn Of The Dons*, A.M. Robertson Company, San Francisco, 1926.

Fox, Helen Morganthau; *Patio Gardens*, MacMillan and Company, New York, 1929.

Garner, Bess Adams; *Windows In An Old Adobe*, Bronson Press, Claremont, CA, 1939.

Garner, William Robert; *Letters From California, 1846-1847* (ed. by D.M. Craig), University of California Press, Berkeley, CA, 1970.

Goytortúa, Jesus; *Pensativa*, F.S. Crofts Company, New York, 1947.

Greentree, Carol; Harriet Barnhart Wimmer: *A Pioneer Woman Landscape Architect*, unpublished paper, University of San Diego, 1986.

Gregory, Daniel; *"Living With Lariats*: Cliff May And Sunset Magazine,"* for a symposium at UCLA, March 5, 1988.

Gross, Susan Jane; *"The Gardens of Edward Huntsman-Trout,"* unpublished graduate thesis, Dept. Of Landscape Architecture, Cal Poly University, Pomona, CA, 1976.

Hanson, Archibald E.; *An Arcadian Landscape: The California Gardens of A.E. Hanson, 1920-32* (edited by David Gebhard), Hennessey and Ingalls, Inc., Los Angeles, 1985.

Hitchcock, Henry-Russell; *"Contemporary Landscape Architecture And Its Sources,"* Contemporary Landscape Architecture, San Francisco Museum of Art, San Francisco, 1937.

Hockaday, Joan; *The Gardens Of San Francisco*, Timber Press, Portland, OR, 1988.

Huntsman-Trout, Edward; *"Another Room In The Home,"* Riverside Plastite Progress, June, 1928.

Keats, John; *The Crack in the Picture Window*, Haughton-Mifflin Company, New York, 1956.

Lehrman, Jonas; *Earthly Paradise*, University of California Press, Berkeley, CA, 1980.

Malnic, Eric; *Los Angeles Times*, June 12, 1990.

Marcus Aurelius; *Meditations (160-180 A.D.)*, Classic Club, New York, 1945.

McDougal, Jane; *Ho For California*! (women's diaries from the Huntington Library.) Edited by Sandra L. Myres, 1980.

Bibliography

Morley, G.L. McCann; (forward), *Contemporary Landscape Architecture And Its Sources*, San Francisco Museum of Art, San Francisco, 1937.

Mott, William Penn, Jr.; *"Parks And Recreation," Landscape Architecture*, San Francisco Museum of Art, San Francisco, 1958.

Nava, Julian and Barger, Robert; *California*, Glencoe Press, Beverly Hills, CA, 1976.

Newcomb, Rexford; *The Old Mission Churches and Historic Houses of California*, J.B. Lippincott, Philadelphia, 1925.

Padilla, Victoria; *Southern California Gardens*, University of California Press, Berkeley, CA, 1961.

Patton, Phil; *"High and Low: Modern Art Meets Popular Culture,"* Smithsonian, November, 1990.

Potter, Stephen C.; *"Introduction to Landscape Design,"* Landscape Design, San Francisco Museum of Art, San Francisco, 1948.

Polyzoides, Stefanos et al; *Courtyard Housing In Los Angeles*, Princeton University Press, New York, 1991.

Pourade, Richard; *Anza Conquers The Desert*, Copley Press, San Diego, 1971.

Rand, Christopher; Los Angeles, *The Ultimate City*, Oxford University Press, New York, 1967.

Ray, Mary Helen and Nichols, Robert P.; *The Traveler's Guide To American Gardens*, University of North Carolina Press, Chapel Hill, N.C., 1988.

Reynolds, Malvina; *"Little Boxes,"* LB Malvina Reynolds, 1956.

Salitore, Evelyn D. (ed.); *California: Past, Present, Future*, Edward V. Salitore Publishing, Lakewood, CA, 1971.

Sanchez, Nellie Van de Grift, *Spanish Arcadia*, Powell Publishing Company, Los Angeles, 1929.

Shipman, Bret; *Old California*, Camaro Company, Los Angeles, 1980.

Simpson, Louis; *"Walt Whitman At Bear Mountain,"* Selected Poems, Harcourt, Brace and World, New York, 1965.

Steele, Fletcher, *"Modern Landscape Architecture,"* Contemporary Landscape Architecture And Its Sources, San Francisco Museum of Art, San Francisco, 1937.

Stewart, Stanley; *The Enclosed Garden*, University of Wisconsin Press, Madison and Milwaukee, 1966.

Thiene, Paul; *"An Old World Garden In A New World Setting,"*, American Landscape Architect, August, 1929.

Tunnard, Christopher; *Gardens In The Modern Landscape* (Revised Edition), Scribner's New York, 1948.

Villiers-Stuart, Constance Mary; *Spanish Gardens*, B.T. Batsford Company, London, 1929.

Wharton, Edith; *Italian Villas And Their Gardens*, Century Company, New York, 1903.

Wilbur, Donald N.; *Persian Gardens And Garden Pavilions*, Charles E. Tuttle and Company, Rutland, VT and Tokyo, 1962.

Wolf, Rex, *Landscaping For Privacy,* Lane Publishing Company (Sunset), Menlo Park, CA, 1985.

Young, Stanley, *The Missions Of California*, Chronicle Books, San Francisco, 1988.

Yoch, James J.; *Landscaping The American Dream: The Gardens And Film Sets Of Florence Yoch*, Sagapress Inc., New York, 1989.

Yoch, James J.; *"Harmony And Invention In The Gardens Of Florence Yoch,"* Pacific Horticulture, Summer, 1989.

Index

Index

Index